Hedonistic Hops
A Hop-Head's Guide to
Kitchen Badassery

Marie Porter

Photography by
Michael Porter

Celebration Generation

www.celebrationgeneration.com

Hedonistic Hops

First Edition, September 2016

I.S.B.N. 978-0-9976608-0-7

Published and Distributed by

Celebration Generation
P.O. Box 22315
Robbinsdale, MN USA
55422

www.celebrationgeneration.com

Cover Photos, Clockwise from Top left:

Hop Infused Dark Chocolate Truffles , page 122
Hoppy IPA Pickles , page 43
Hoppy Citrus IPA Wings, page 66
Hoppy Citrus French Macarons , page 133
Lemonade , page 144

Back Cover Photo:

Jerk Chicken, page72

Acknowledgments

As always, major props to my husband, Michael Porter.

As with all of my books, he has contributed gorgeous photography, recipe testing, and constant, unwavering support for the project.

This time around has been even more hands-on for him, as it was his love for hops that inspired this project. He helped educate me on hops, grew, harvested, and preserved our hops, gave input on recipes we should create, and was advisor as to what types of hops would work best for each application.

This was my second cookbook project to come to fruition as the result of a crowd funding campaign!

My sincerest thanks to everyone who contributed to the Kickstarter project financially, and also to those who spread the word and encouraged others to have a look at the campaign. I hope you love the fruit of your generosity!

In particular, I'd like to thank the following establishments for spreading the word to their followings:

Beer Grains Supply Co.
Brew UK Limited
Canadian Homebrew Supplies
Canuck Homebrew Supply
Centennial Homebrewing Supplies
Dry Dock Brewing Co.
Ferment Station
Food Bloggers of Canada
Gorst Valley Hops
Oregon Hop Commission
Seven Bridges Organic Brewing Supply
The Beer Essentials
The Brewstore ltd (UK)

Table of Contents

Foreword

I'll be the first to admit it - I don't like to drink beer. Certain, more mild kinds are great as cooking ingredients, in my opinion - but that's about it. I find the hoppier beers that my husband likes to be completely obnoxious.

... how ironic is it that I ended up writing this book?

This cookbook actually started way back in 2010, though I didn't realize it at the time. My husband was harvesting his first crop of backyard hops, and I'd been on a truffle making kick.

I had decided to steep some of his freshly picked hops in heavy cream while making a batch of dark chocolate truffles for him - "Bitter is better" is his motto.. and he loved them.

The next day, I invented "LolliHOPS" - A hop flavoured beer lollipop, which also went over spectacularly well with everyone who tried them. Even *I* liked them!

... it was an idea AND name that were both snatched from my food blog a few years later, by a small company who went on to produce a variation of it... to my dismay. On the bright side, it showed that it really was a great idea!

A few months later, our lives were kind of derailed when we were hit by a tornado. I'm still shocked that our hop plants managed to survive - we were surprised to see the shoots coming back up after we pulled a ton of debris off them... and then again after they were tramped down to nothing by the roofers. Hops are extremely resilient plants, once they get going!

The idea of cooking with hops took a backseat to life, for a while.

In 2014, one of our hophead friends came by to help harvest a HUGE season of hops with my husband, while I was on cooking duty.

I decided to make them some food flavoured with hops - A BBQ sauce, and hoppy citrus IPA glazed wings. Oh, they were *fabulous*. The idea for a cookbook was born!

As someone with an alphabetically-arranged spice rack that now tops 80 pieces, I soon got past my dislike of beer to get to know hops on their own. I'm always looking for new flavours, new combinations, and new things to play with. Cooking should be fun, not a chore!

The hops did not disappoint. I discovered that - Much like salt or lemon juice can be added to dishes to perk them up - Hops can similarly elevate a dish. A small amount of hops - used wisely, and with specific techniques to do so in a balanced fashion - can really make a dish sing. This is especially true when supporting ingredients and techniques are selected to kill the *bitter* of the hops, allowing for the flavours and aromas of the hops to shine through.

Even those who are not fans of beer will love the unique flavours that various types of hops can bring to their plate. Floral, earthy, peppery, citrusy... Cooking with hops is a great way to expand your seasoning arsenal.

We had a blast brainstorming and developing recipes, and here we are!

I hope you enjoy these recipes as much as we do!

- Marie Porter

Let's Get it Started

Before we get going on the various ways you can use hops in cooking, let's address what hops are.

"Hops" are the cone shaped flowers of the hop plant - *Humulus lupulus* - a member of the Cannabaceae family, and a climbing perennial bine . As a quick (Very quick. Damn it Jim, this is a cookbook, not a history text!) history:

Hops have been cultivated for over 1000 years, with the earliest documented cultivation occurring in Germany in the 700s. In the centuries that followed, hops have been taxed, banned, imported, exported, and celebrated all over Europe... eventually being cultivated in North America starting in the 1600s.

These days, hops are grown in abundance in many areas, with the Germany, the Pacific Northwest of the USA, China, Australia, and certain areas of the UK being among the world leaders in production.

Anatomy of a Hop Plant

While hop flowers themselves get all the glory, they're not the only useful parts of a hop plant - and certainly not the only part you'll need to know about if you want to get into growing them yourself!

First of all, hops grow on a bine, not a vine. Sure, the terms get used interchangeably all the time, but there are some key differences. The biggest difference is the manner in which they climb - vines "grab" with curly tendrils they shoot out, while bines use stiff little hairs to aid in wrapping themselves around whatever they can - Usually long poles and/or hanging rope or twine, but also trees, other plants, fences, etc - to "climb" up in a spiral fashion.

The main parts of a hop plant are:

Rhizome: While some plants start from seeds, or from bulbs.. Hops are planted in the form of a rhizome. It looks like a twig, and is planted horizontally. From the rhizome, "roots" (more rhizomes) grow downward, and hop shoots grow upward. As a rhizome matures - after a season or so - it becomes a "crown" - an established "root" ball, which should be trimmed every 3-4 years or so.

Shoots: The very first appearance of the hop plant in the spring. Shoots are tasty to eat, but only for a few weeks at the beginning of each season!

Bine: The shoots become bines - long, twisting vine-like plants, covered in tiny hairs. After the harvest, these can be gathered, trimmed, and twisted into rustic decorations - like wreaths - and dried. Waste not!

Leaves: The leaves serve two main purposes: To soak up the sun for nourishment, and - to some degree - to protect the hop flowers from the sun. The leaves are also tasty, and can be used in much the same way as grape leaves.

Buds: The start of a hop flower

Flowers: The main point of growing hops! Used 'wet' or dried, the various acids and essential oils contribute flavour, aroma, bitterness, and preservative qualities to beer, and other items. Hops are also used for calming teas, and certain alternative medicines.

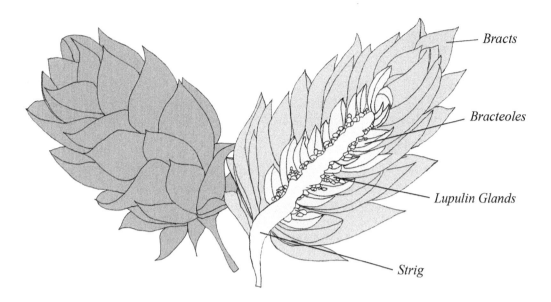

Bracteoles: Smaller versions of the bracts, located towards the inside of the flower. The bracteoles cover/contain the lupulin glands.

Bracts: Delicate little outer "leaves" that form the bulk of the flower, these cover and protect the bracteoles and lupulin glands.

Lupulin Glands: Where the lupulin is produced and concentrated; a sticky yellow substance, resembling pollen. This is where most of the chemicals that hops are prized for are contained - alpha acids, beta acids, and essentially oils, most importantly.

Strig: The core and "stem" of the hop flower, connecting it to the actual bine. This is where most of the tannins / polyphenols in the plant are located.

On Acid...

The acids contained in lupulin fall into one of two main categories: Alpha acids and Beta acids.

Alpha Acids:

Alpha acids are where the bulk of the bittering properties come from, which is important to consider when choosing hops for cooking with. Too bitter, and you'll ruin a dish!

When it comes to beer making, hops high in alpha acids are typically used in the initial boil, for a fairly long amount of time. The boiling draws out the acids into the wort (beer before it becomes beer!), through a chemical reaction called "isomerization". These hops are commonly referred to as "bittering hops".

Alpha acids are the reason that hops came into favour as a preservative agent, as they have antimicrobial qualities - preventing the growth of bacteria, while not hampering the ability of yeast to grow and ferment the beer.

The primary alpha acids are:

Cohumulone -   The bitterness that comes from cohumulone is known to be a "harsher" bitterness, not as refined tasting as the bitterness that comes from Humulone.

Humulone -   This is the main bittering acid - it gets bitter when boiled. It's known for a less "harsh" bitter. Hops with high alpha levels with most of the alpha acids coming from humulone are considered a good thing.

The other alpha acids include adhumulone, posthumulone, prehumulone. The attributes of those acids aren't as well known, and generally aren't really addressed when brewing beer - or cooking with hops.

Alpha acids are also the reason that beers tend to be sold in brown bottles and in cans - when exposed to both the riboflavin in the wort and sunlight, alpha acids go off, creating a skunky smell.

Beta Acids:

Beta acids work a bit differently, when it comes to the bittering of beer. Rather than their bitterness coming out in a long boil, their aroma and bitterness comes from more long term application, usually in dry hopping, or while aging beer. The changes come as a result of the acids breaking down. Oxidization, rather than through isomerization.

Much like alpha acids, beta acids also have great antiseptic qualities.

The primary beta acids are Adlupulone, Colupulone, and Lupulone.

Noble Hops

Noble hops are a group of hops with low alpha acids. They're used for flavouring less intense beers, rather than offering a lot of bitterness.

Because of the lower acid levels - and lower bitterness, as a result! - the Noble hops are great for getting into cooking with hops. They're not as finicky or daring to use.

The main Noble Hops are:

Hallertauer: A German hop, "floral" and "spicy".

Tettnanger: A German hop, "fruity" and "spicy"

Spalt: A German hop, similar to Hallertauer: "floral" and "spicy"

Saaz: A Czech hop, "floral" with a slight bit of "spicy"

Noble hops aren't the only hops with low Alpha acids, however. English Fuggles, East Kent Golding, Liberty, Mt Hood, Styrian Golding, Vanguard, Willamette are just a few that are considered to be ALMOST "Noble".

IBU / EBU

IBU refers to "International Bittering Units", EBU refers to "European Bittering Units" - a value given to finished beers, based on the amount of alpha acid tested to be present in the beer.

Good information to know - it certainly helps me when selecting gift beer for my husband! - but for the purposes of cooking, it's not really relevant .

"Aromatic" vs "Bittering"

As hops are rated by their bitterness, this rating is used to - for the most part - determine the function of a hop. Hops high in alpha acids are generally considered to be "bittering" hops, while hops low in alpha acid are used more for their aromas and flavours - and thus, are "aromatic hops".

Essential Oils

Where acids contribute the bitterness to hop flavouring, essential oils contribute aromas and actual flavour. When you see descriptors of "Citrus", "Earthy" "Floral", "Fruity", "Grassy", "Herbal", "Piney" and "Spicy" - these are referring to the flavours contributed by the essential oils in each variety of hops.

These oils work pretty much the opposite of the alpha acids, in terms of extraction. Alpha acids need a long boil, while essential oils are boiled off and lost in long boils. For this reason, hops being used for aroma are added in the last few minutes of a boil, or in dry hopping.

Aroma Profiles

With all this talk of acids and essential oils, let's look at some popular hop varieties, and what you can expect from them.

First of all, there are hundreds of hop varieties out there. Some may be popular everywhere, others may be more regional. Some are easier to come by than others. Some you have to buy as finished hops, as the growing of them is proprietary and protected by licenses.

So, for various reasons, this is not an exhaustive list - more like a starting point. See what's readily available in your area, get a feel for what you love. Once you've gotten into it, you can get creative with obtaining hops - ordering online, swapping with home growers, etc!

Amarillo® :   A bittering hop, with 7-11% acid. Floral / Citrus aroma.

Bramling Cross: A dual purpose hop, at 5-7% acid. Fruity and mild aromas of black currant, lemon, and spice.

Cascade: One of the most popular hops, this is an aroma hop with 4.5-7% acid. Citrus and Floral, with hints of grapefruit and spice.

Centennial: Primarily a bittering hop, but also used as an aromatic, with 9.5-11.5% acid. Very similar to both Cascade and Chinook, citrus aroma.

Chinook: Another dual purpose hop, used for both bittering and aromatics. 12-14% acid, piney and spicy aromas.

Columbus: A bittering hop, but also used for aroma. 14-18% acid, citrus aromas.

Citra ®:   Citra® is a registered, trademarked hop variety... and my favourite for cooking with. This is a bittering hop at 12-16% acid. Because of the high acid, I prefer to use this for making extracts, rather than actually cooking with outright. Very fruity - mostly citrus. Makes an amazing cheesecake.

Crystal: Crystal is an aromatic hop, with 3.5-6% acid. It's floral and spicy, with notes of black pepper and cinnamon.

Falconer's Flight 7 Cs® :   Another trademarked hop.. Sort of. This is a proprietary blend of hops - 7 of them, all starting with "C" - available in pellet form. Used for bittering, it's at 9.5-12% acid, with strong fruity and citrus aromas. Really nice as an extract.

Fuggle: Fuggles are an aromatic hop, with 3.5-5.5% acid. Earthy aromas, Fuggles go really well with chocolate desserts and meat dishes.

Galaxy: Dual purpose Australian hop, with 11-16% alpha acid. Very fruity, with citrus, passionfruit, and peach aromas. One of my husband's favourites, when it comes to beer. One of my favourites, when it comes to dessert making!

Green Bullet: Bittering hop from New Zealand, with 11-14% alpha acid. Fruity, spicy, and grassy.

Equinox®: Flavour/aroma hop, with 13-16% acid. A newer hop, this one has a complex aroma -floral, herbal, and tropical fruit aromas, with a touch of cedar. A fun one!

Hallertauer: A German "noble" hop, 3.5-5.5% acid. Floral, herbal, and spicy notes.

Huell Melon: A mellow, aromatic hop with distinct fruity aromas, including melon, peach and .. strawberry? 6.5-7.5% acid.

Kent Goulding: Aromatic hop with 4-5.5% acid. Floral and earthy with a bit of citrus and spice.

Liberty: An aromatic, "noble" hop, 3-5% acid, notes of spice.

Mosaic®: Dual purpose hop, but usually aromatic. Fruity, earthy and a bit of pine. 11-13% acid.

Mt. Hood: Aromatic hop, 4-7% acid. Mild aromas of florals and spice.

Nelson Sauvin: Dual purpose hop, at 12-14% alpha acid. Known for having flavours of fruit and white wine.

Northern Brewer: Dual purpose, 8-12% acid. Earthy and woody, with a bit of pine.

Pacific Jade: Dual purpose hop at 12-14% acid. Citrussy with black pepper notes. A great all around hop to cook with. Use as an extract if worried about bitterness.

Pride of Ringwood: Primarily a bittering hop, with 7-10% acid. Woody, earthy, and spicy.

Saaz: Aromatic, "noble" hop at 4.5% acid. Earthy and spicy.

Sorachi Ace: Dual purpose hop, 10-16% acid. Unique flavour profile: citrussy and dill!

Spalt: A German "noble" aromatic hop, similar to Hallertauer, 4-6% acid. Floral and spicy characteristics.

Sterling: Dual purpose hop, 6-9% acid. Citrus, herbal, and spicy, hint of floral.

Styrian Golding: An "almost noble" aromatic hop, and 4.5-6% acid. Mildly spicy aroma.

Summit®:   Bittering hop, 17-19% acid. Earthy, citrus, and onion/garlic aromas.

Tettnanger: A German "noble" hop, 3.5-5.5% acid. Herbal and spicy aromas.

Willamette: Aromatic hop, at 4-6% acid. Known for its smooth blend of earthy, floral, fruit, and spice aromas.

Vanguard: Another "Almost noble" aromatic hop at 4-5.5% acid. Mild aroma of spice.

Purchase, Storage, and Use of Hops

Buying Hops

Hops can be purchased year round, through any homebrew store. You can even order them online, shipped right to your door! They come in the following forms:

Pellets: Pelletized hops are made from milling hops into a powder, before being heated, pressed, run through an extrusion process, and cooled. They're sold chilled, and in mylar bags. They take up far less space than a similar weight of leaf hops, and also stay fresher longer.

Dried or "Leaf" Hops: These are hops that were dried shortly after being harvested. They are stored in freezers or coolers, and are usually sold by weight, in mylar bags. Bags tend to contain a mix of whole cones, and loose leaves. (Dried hop cones are very fragile, and will split into loose leaves VERY easily).

Fresh: Fresh off the bine hops are far less available than dried or pelletized hops, and are only available seasonally. In my opinion, those looking to utilize fresh hops are usually best off either growing them, or knowing someone who does.

Storing Hops

No matter the format you're using, there are a few natural "enemies" of your hops - Heat, oxygen, and light. The better you can protect your hops from these elements, the longer they will taste right.

Time is also a natural enemy of hops - the alpha acids and essential oils begin degrading almost as soon as the hops are picked from the bine - but the damage that time brings can be mitigated with careful attention paid to the aforementioned elements.

Store your hops chilled, in dark, airtight containers. Mylar/foil bags are great at preventing light damage. If your hops don't come in resealable bags, you can buy stand up pouches from many places online. We'll usually buy a pack of 200, and use them for several harvests worth of hops.

While we usually just press out most of the air as we're sealing the bags, vacuum seal bags are also a great option, especially if you'll be storing your hops for more than a few months. As most vacuum seal bags are clear, it's a good idea to store vacuum packed hops in a second, darker bag or container.

For hops you'll be using within a few days, refrigerator storage is fine . If you're looking to store for much longer than that, storing them in the freezer is the best way to go.

While heat, oxygen, and light can be kept at bay with your packaging and storage, time is still an issue. Freezing slows the degradation of alpha acids and essential oils, but doesn't stop it. For that reason, we recommend throwing out hops after a year in the freezer.

They won't be BAD after a year in the freezer, much the same way that spices are *bad* after a year or two... it's just nicest to just use fresher ones!

Using Hops in Cooking

When using hops in brewing, the process is pretty much universal - You put the hops in the boiling wort at some point (either for a long boil, or for aromatics at the end), and strain the hops out at some point. This is the case whether using fresh, dried, or pelletized hops.

When it comes to cooking with hops, the method really depends on the type of hop, as well as the type of recipe. You can use any form of hop, strain it out or leave it in, etc.

As discussed earlier, boiling hops isomerizes the alpha acids, bringing out the bitterness. This applies to cooking as well as brewing! Unless you're really looking to highlight bitter flavours, hops should be added towards the end of any boiling involved with a dish.

Also, a cheat note: A small amount of baking soda and/or sugar can neutralize and balance out a bit of the bitter, if you go a bit too nuts with the hops!

Infusion: Hops can be used to infuse a dish, then strained out - for instance, when making sauces, custards, etc. This is great for when you want the flavour of the hops, but without actual hop material in the dish.

You can infuse/strain any format of hop - fresh, dried, pelletized - but the straining out will differ. A normal sieve / colander will work great for fresh or dried hops, but to remove bits of pelletized hops, it's best to line your sieve with a layer of fine cheese cloth.

Another issue to take into account is liquid uptake. Fresh hops will remove little - if any - liquid from your recipe. Dried hops will reconstitute slightly, removing a bit of the liquid from your dish.

Pelletized hops, however, take up a significant amount of liquid in reconstitution. You can squeeze some of this liquid out of the pulp during the straining step, but it will hold onto a fair amount. If you're using pelletized hops in a recipe that calls for dried or fresh hop leaves, you may want to add a bit more liquid to compensate for the liquid retained by the hop pulp.

Grinding: Sometimes I'll use hops in such a way that I don't plan to remove them from the dish. To better distribute the flavours throughout the dish, the pieces of hop need to be broken down into a finer texture.

For this, I'll use a mortar and pestle (pellet hops), or a spice/coffee grinder. This works best with dried and pellet hops (you can get them down to a fine powder), but will also do a good job of shredding fresh hops down to smaller pieces as well.

Whole Leaf: Sometimes, having the whole "leaves" (bracts) of the hop flower in a recipe can be desirable, even pretty. This is usually best done with dried hops, as they break down into individual leaves much more easily than fresh hops. While my husband would be more than happy to have entire hop cones in his food, MOST people would not find that palatable!

Whole Flower: Very rarely, I'll use whole hop flowers in cooking. Generally speaking, this would be for applications where I like the visual of a whole hop... and have the opportunity to do so in a way where the hop isn't necessarily part of the food to be eaten. Basically? Pickling. I like the look of whole hop flowers in our hop pickle jars! For this kind of use, fresh hops are best - dried hops break apart too easily.

Extracts: One of the most convenient ways to include hop flavouring into your cooking and baking is through the use of homemade* hop extracts, which are very easy to make.

The only ingredient aside from hops is just a neutral alcohol base. This alcohol extracts flavours/ aromas from the hop, without the isomerization of the alpha acids. Any good quality vodka will work.

I like to keep a few extracts on hand - usually one that's more citrussy, one that's more herbal, etc. My go-to for cooking/baking is my Citra® hop extract. LOVE it. Unlike normal baking extracts - which are normally used exclusively for sweet applications - you can use hop extracts in almost anything - sweet or savoury!

Hop Extract

While I'm a purist and like to have single hop extracts, you can have a lot of fun with mixing hop varieties to come up with new favourite flavours.

Good quality vodka	2 cups	500 ml
Fresh hops, gently rinsed	1 cup	250 ml
OR		
Dry hop leaves	3/4 cup	175 ml
OR		
Pellet hops	2 Tbsp	30 ml

Place hops of choice into a large, clean mason jar. Pour vodka over the hops, cap with a clean, tight fitting lid. Give the jar a good shake, store in a cool dark place. Shake the jar a couple times daily for about a week.

After about a week, taste for doneness. You're looking for a potent extract, much like vanilla or lemon extract. It's not supposed to be drinkable!

Once desired flavour strength is achieved, strain the extract. I like to strain the infusion first with a fine mesh strainer, then a second time through a coffee filter. I find this results in the cleanest, clearest finished extract. Bottle the strained extract into clear - ideally dark - bottles.

* Please note: While commercially available hop extracts are available, they are NOT the same as baking extracts. They have different chemical processes and ingredients applied to them - sometimes to force isomerization - where these are just a pure extraction.

Finished hop extracts, after straining

Growing Your Own Hops

If you live in one of the many areas where hops can flourish - between the 35-55 parallels of both the northern and southern hemispheres - consider growing them at home. They're easy, hardy, and can make a pretty addition to your house/garden.

Just a couple months after planting hops at our new house, we were hit by a tornado, and those brand new hop plants were covered in about 5' of debris. Then, they were trampled by clean up and relief efforts... and they came back! I'm not kidding when I say that they're hardy plants!

Planning Your Planting:

What: Generally speaking, hop plants are sold as rhizomes - small cuttings from an established crown. Sometimes you can find whole crowns available for sale as well. Whether rhizome or crown, these are generally only available during planting season.

Once you receive your rhizome or crown, place it in a plastic baggie, mist it with a little water, and refrigerate until you plant it - you should definitely plan to plant it ASAP after receiving it.

Who: Hop rhizomes can be purchased from most/all home brew supply stores, from some private hop growers, and even from some farmers markets. Additionally, many homebrew enthusiasts will trade / give away rhizomes when it's time to split their own.

No matter which way you go, it's good to decide where you're going to be getting your hops from ahead of time, as they can sell out fast.

When: Hops need to be planted in the spring, soon after the ground thaws. They'll survive a frost after planting, but you won't want to subject them to a full ground freeze until after they've been established. In North America, hop planting season tends to be from March to May.

Where: Hops do best in full sun, so planting on the south side of your house is ideal. (I would assume this would be north side, in the southern hemisphere?). Hops can spread like crazy, so be sure to allow a fair amount of room.

In terms of soil, hops aren't super picky. Hops flourish in sandy soils with good drainage. Drainage is definitely more important than the type of soil - poorly drained soil should be avoided altogether.

Another consideration for the "where" of planting is the vertical growth - You'll want to have 15-20' of vertical space available for growth. Hops require twine, rope, a trellis, or other vertical structures to climb up.

For us, this is achieved by tying long ropes of twine to our second floor mini deck, and letting them dangle over the hop garden below. Our first year, we secured the ends to the ground with tent stakes, but high winds soon pulled them out. We kept replacing them, only to have them blown out again. In the end, it didn't matter: The hops will grab them and climb, securing them in the process.

Nowadays, we don't bother staking the ends at all - though we will wind the early shoots around the ends of the twine - once they're a few feet long - to encourage climbing. Good to set them off in the right direction!

Depending on your house and yard, you can:

- Install eye hooks to roof overhangs, trim, tall decks, balconies, etc. We find this is the best method. Just hang some twine from the hooks, and you have an quick, easy installation that is the easiest to harvest. Just be sure that your setup is able to hold a fair amount of weight - mature hop plants can weigh 20 lbs or more!

- Tie twine from the spindles or posts of tall decks / balconies, allowing them to fall all the way to the ground below. Also a very quick, easy installation that is very easy to harvest from.

- Tie twine to strong branches of tall trees - just make sure they'll still be in a sunny location, not completely shaded by the tree!

- Affix trellis to an exterior wall, and allow the bines to climb it. This can be more of a pain to harvest from, however, due to the way they grow into it.

Finally, consider overhead drainage. Don't plant your hops anywhere that receives a lot of water drainage from your house. Down spouts, overhangs, etc. Take note of where the water falls and pools when it rains, avoid those spots.

How:

Ideally, till the ground you'll be planting the hops into. This loosens it up, so they can more easily establish themselves.

Plant the rhizome 4" deep into the soil, laying horizontally. Space rhizomes several feet away from each other : 3+ feet for the same variety, and 5+ feet between different varieties. If planted too close together, hop plants become more susceptible to issues like mildew. Give them some space, let them do their thing.

Give them a light watering when you plant them, and a light watering every few days the first few months -assuming it hasn't been raining.. You do NOT want them sitting around in puddles - hop plants aren't fans of a lot of water, so don't overdo it. Water in the mornings or early afternoons, so the plants can dry off during the day. Too much water will cause the roots to rot and die.

The first hop shoots of the season

As the hop shoots start to grow, decide on a few strong growers per plant, and trim the rest back. I know, it's tempting to just let them all grow - like all you can think about is the hops you'll be missing out on by trimming! - but only allowing a few bines per plant ensures that they'll be healthy, get a lot of nutrients, and not be overcrowded.

- Once the chosen few bines are 2-3 feet tall, gently wrap them around your rope, twine, or trellis. You may need to do this more than once, especially if it gets windy. Generally speaking, though, they will grip pretty well after a couple of days.

- Throughout the season, keep the area tidy. Weed frequently, and cut back any new shoots that pop up from the ground.

Left to their own devices, hops will grow like weeds, and take over any area!

Cooking with Hop Shoots

After a year or two of growing hops, you'll find yourself trimming back a lot of shoots - which you can eat! Hop shoots are actually known to be the most expensive "vegetable" in the world, sometimes commanding upwards of $1500/lb.

... and you were just going to compost those precious shoots, weren't you?

They're popular as a vegetable in pockets of Europe. This is especially true in Italy, where hop shoots are known as "Bruscandoli", and are popular in frittata and risotto.

In North America, people are JUST starting to use hop shoots in cooking. The most popular use of hop shoots in the USA is to pickle them and use them as a snack or flavourful garnish. (You can find our Pickled Hop Shoots recipe on page 47)

Hop shoots are best harvested early in the year, when they're under 5" tall. Exposure to the elements - especially the sun - toughens up the tender shoots.

Hops shoots can be eaten raw - try them in a salad - or blanched for a minute to heat and soften them slightly. Dress raw or blanched hop shoots with a light vinaigrette, or use them in place of asparagus in almost any recipe.

Personally, my favourite preparation is to just sautee them with a little butter, salt, and pepper.

Very early hop shoots. Tasty!

26

Pests and Disease

Like most garden plants, pests and disease can negatively impact the development of your hops. Keep an eye on things, and address any issues ASAP after they start up. The most common issues for hops are:

Aphids: Tiny, pale green bugs that hang out on the undersides of the leaves. Easily visible to the naked eye, these can be dealt with by using natural pesticides (available wherever you buy your rhizomes), or by introducing ladybugs to the area. Ladybugs love to eat aphids, and can be purchased at many garden centers, or even online.

Mildew: There are two main types of mildew that impact hop plants: Downy mildew and powdery mildew. Both are common to over watered hop plants, and both can be devastating to your crop.

    Downy Mildew: This mildew is more varied in presentation - discoloured leaves, curled leaves, black spots on leaves (spores). Leaves turn yellow or brown and die quickly - sometimes even before the fungus itself is apparent. This mildew is more common in cooler climates.

    Powdery Mildew: This type of fungus resembles a white powder on the undersides of leaves. This mildew is more common in moderate climates, and is the most common mildew to affect hops.

The best way to deal with mildew is to prevent it in the first place: Watering early in the day, don't over- water, avoid crowding, keep the area clear of extra growth and weeds.

If you find yourself dealing with a mildew issue, trim off the affected areas and dispose of them in the garbage. Do NOT allow affected leaves to remain close to your hop plants, and don't compost them.

Once visibly infected areas are removed, treat your plans with a gardening fungicide.

Spider Mites: Much smaller than aphids, you're less likely to see them with your naked eye. You're more likely to notice very fine spider webbing on the leaves, combined with spotty, discoloured leaves . Spider mites are usually controlled with the same pesticides as aphids - or, again, with ladybugs.

Harvesting Your Hops

Hops are generally ready to harvest in the late summer or very early fall. For us, that's usually mid September, but depending on your area, it could be anywhere from August to October. (Northern Hemisphere, anyway - your mileage will vary GREATLY in the southern hemisphere!)

As you get closer to the typical harvesting season, make a point of checking in on your hops daily. Give a few a little squeeze - as hops "ripen", they'll lose their moisture and become almost papery. You may also notice some slight browning.

When the bulk of your hops have reached this delicate, papery stage, you should plan to harvest ASAP. With their moisture levels reduced, they're even more susceptible to scorching from the sun.

Harvesting day is a bit of an event for us - we have a ton of hops, so it's a fair amount of work. We have our friend Trevor - a hop head - over for the afternoon. While the two of them spend hours picking hops off the bines, I'll be cooking lunch and dinner for them. It's a good time to experiment with hop cooking - and may have actually been the genesis of this book!

Everyone is going to have their own routine for harvesting. Here is how we do it:

- Early on harvest day, we'll clean off our large patio table in the back yard, and do a good sweep of the patio itself. It's best to harvest outdoors, as the bines can house many bugs.

- We'll dig out and wash a couple of large, food grade buckets, and make sure that we have compost leaf bags on hand. These are great to work with, as they have a large, flat bottom and stand / stay open on their own.

- Those harvesting the hops will wear long sleeved shirts. Hop bines can cause some wicked contact dermatitis, so it's best to just avoid that. Thin work gloves are a good idea also - you want the dexterity to pick hops, but also have a little bit of a protection from them.

- One plant at a time, we'll cut down the rope/twine, and bring a whole plant worth of hops over to the patio table - leaving about 1 foot of bine at the ground. The guys will pick through the hop bines, putting the healthy, good looking hops in the food grade buckets.

- Any hops that are overly browned get tossed out. With the massive amounts of hops we harvest from even a plant or two, it's not worth it to keep less than awesome hops.

- As bines are stripped of the hops on them, they are tossed on a pile to be composted. Alternately, you can save them to make hop bine wreaths and other crafts.

- As buckets are filled, they are dumped into a large brown paper composting bag, which is labeled with the variety of hop contained.

- All of the plants for one variety are harvested before moving on to the other varieties. Once a variety is done and all the harvested hops are transferred to the composting bag, the bag is lightly folded shut and set aside.

- A new bag is labeled for the next variety, lather, rinse, and repeat.

Just a note for first time growers: Your first year will probably produce a small amount of hops, so try not to be underwhelmed. Your yield will increase greatly over the second and third years.

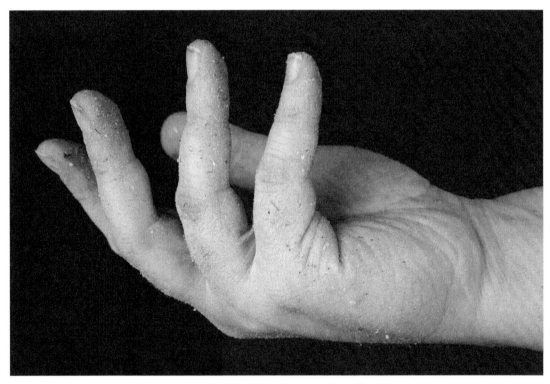

Working with hops can be messy - lupulin is sticky!

Preserving Hops

Before harvest, we dig out our food dehydrator, and make arrangements to borrow a few more. You want to take all of your hops from "fresh off the bine" to dehydrated, sealed, and chilled as quickly as possible. When you have several dehydrators going at once, it can go very quickly!

Working with one bag / variety of hops at a time, spread your hops out on your dehydrator trays. Don't worry about crowding - they're so airy and papery, they can be lightly piled in there.

We find that it takes about 8 hours in the dehydrator for them to be completely dry - and this is the case across the different models of dehydrators we tend to have on hand. (Basically, whatever we can get our hands on for a few days!). We'll time it so we start new batches first thing in the morning, in the afternoon, and before bed. Only dry your hops long enough to be DRY - over drying will start to degrade the alpha acids and essential oils.

Start a fresh new - labeled - compost bag for each variety of hops to be held in as they're dried, and fold it closed after each new addition of dried hops. You'll want to protect them from moisture and light as you finish all the hops of that variety.

Once all of your hops have been dried, you'll want to package them.

We like to use 12oz size foil standing pouches. We weigh 2oz of dried hops into each bag, squeeze all the air out, zipper them shut, and then seal with a heat sealer. All bags are labeled with hop variety and harvest year, and go straight into the chest freezer in our brew room.

Vacuum seal bags are also a great idea, so long as you transfer the sealed bags - usually clear - to dark bags to block the light.

Preserving Hop Leaves

Hop leaves are delicious, especially early on in the hop growth cycle - and there are several recipes that use them in this book. To be able to use hop leaves year round, though, you'll want to preserve some.

Hop leaves are best harvested when they're just starting to each the size of your hand - This will be when they're not only the right size, but still tender and undamaged by the sun and grasshoppers. They should be free of discolouration, holes, and signs of mildew.

This recipe is for 1 jar, and can be multiplied for as many leaves as you'd like to preserve.

Canned Hop Leaves

Hop leaves	50	50
Water	4 cups	1000 ml
Salt	1 Tbsp	15 ml
Water	1 ½ cups	375 ml
Vinegar	1/3 cup	75 ml

Equipment:
Clean, sterilized 1 quart canning jar(s) & ring(s)
Canning funnel
New, never-used, sterilized canning lid(s)
LARGE pot to process in
Smaller pot
Jar lifter

Wash leaves off twice, trim any excess stem. Fill your LARGE pot with at least 6" of water, put on medium or high heat to bring it to a boil as you prepare your leaves and brine.

In a separate pot, bring water and salt to a boil, blanch leaves for about 2 minutes. Strain water off, allow to cool enough to handle.

Stack leaves in piles of 10, roll them up and place in a sterilized 1 quart wide mouth mason jar. Fit jar with canning funnel.

Bring water and vinegar to a boil, pour over leaves, leaving 1/4" head space. Tap the jar a few times to settle the water in between the leaves, top up with more water as needed.

Wipe off the top edges of the jar with a clean, wet towel, top each with a new, sterilized lid, and carefully screw on a clean lid ring. I like to use a kitchen towel for this, the jars are HOT! Carefully place into the boiling water pot, allow to process for 15 minutes. Carefully remove them, allow to cool overnight.

The next morning, check to make sure that all of the jars achieved a proper seal – try to push down in the middle of each lid. If it "pops", it did not seal. Any jars that didn't seal should be put in the fridge and used in the next few weeks.

Jars that sealed properly can be stored in a cool dark place for up to a year. To use the leaves, simply unroll as many stacks as you'd like, and soak in cool water for 5-10 minutes.

Canned Hop Leaves

Frozen Hop Leaves

Hop leaves	50-100	50-100
Water	4 cups	1000 ml
Salt	1 Tbsp	15 ml

Wash leaves off twice, trim any excess stem.

In a separate pot, bring water and salt to a boil, blanch leaves for about 2 minutes. Strain water off, spread on paper towels, and allow to cool enough to handle.

Stack leaves in piles of 10, roll them up tightly, and pack into good quality freezer bags. If you'd like to secure each roll with kitchen twine, you can - I don't usually bother.

Squeeze / vacuum as much air out of the freezer bags as possible. Seal, and freeze for up to a year.

To use, simply defrost in the fridge, or by immersing freezer bag in hot water for a few minutes.

Hop Bine Crafting

So, this is definitely not an edible thing, but in the spirit of "waste not want not", and preserving different parts of the hop plants you've been growing... figure I may as well touch on it.

After harvesting your hops, hop bines can be used for crafting, in the exact same way that grape vines are. You can create all kinds of rustic pieces: wreaths, baskets, swags, sculptures, and various hanging pieces.

If you know you'll want to give it a go, just trim the bines as much as possible, after harvesting the hops. Remove all leaves, and any "branches", shoots, etc that you don't want. Use immediately, or spread the trimmed bines out to dry.

To use later, soak in boiling water for 10 minutes, or until supple. If you're soaking a LOT of bines, fill your bathtub with bines, cover with the hottest water you can, and allow to soak for about an hour.

Cruise pinterest for "grapevine crafts" ideas, craft your heart out, and then allow your finished piece to completely dry out.

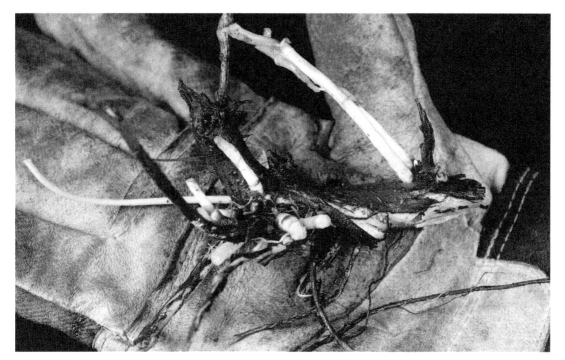

Piece of rhizome, with several shoots

Splitting Hop Crowns

After the first two years of growing, you'll notice that hops can get VERY unruly. The rhizomes spread underground, and need to be trimmed back every 3-4 years or so. Much like other types of rhizome or bulb plants that grow the same way, splitting the rhizomes not only keep things tidier, it aids in keeping your hop crown healthy and efficient!

In the spring - when the ground has thawed and the shoots haven't started coming up yet - carefully dig up your hop crown. 3 years is a long time for hop growth, so expect that it will have spread a significant amount. Try to carefully dig up as much as you can in one piece - any roots/rhizome that gets cut off and left in the ground can potentially grow a whole new plant!

Look for a few long rhizomes that have buds / shoots / "eyes" on them - these are the best for trimming off. Cut off long sections of rhizome, and split each into multiple sections - try to have one bud / shoot per section.

Immediately plant your root ball where / how it was located, with the shoots aiming upwards.

Plant your new rhizomes immediately, or mist with water, place in zipper bags, and chill in your fridge until you're ready to use them. Swapping rhizome cuts with fellow home growers can be a fun way to increase the variety of the hops you grow - just be sure to leave plenty of room between different varieties!

Now.. let's cook!

Porterhouse Guacamole

Appetizers & Sides

Porterhouse Guacamole

The bite of the hops really compliments the creamy, fatty mouth feel of the avocado. The grassy, citrussy overtones from the hops work well with the whole vegetable mix, and could even substitute for cilantro for those who don't like cilantro.

As with most guacamole recipes, this is highly adaptable. You can trim the seeds and ribs from the jalapeno for less heat, or add more jalapenos for more heat. Toss in a chopped up mango for even more colour, and to up the sweetness if you like – it's really quite flexible!

We use red pepper in our guacamole, as my husband *hates* tomato. Feel free to substitute tomatoes, if you wish.

I prefer to use hop extract for this, but you can use fresh or dried hop leaves instead. 2 tsp (10 ml) of shredded dried hops or 1 Tbsp (15 ml) of shredded fresh hops work well as a start!

Makes about 4 cups

Ripe avocados, seeded and peeled	5	5
Lime, zested and juiced	1	1
Red bell pepper, seeded and chopped	1	1
Red onion, chopped	½	½
Jalapeno peppers, finely chopped	2	2
Garlic cloves, pressed or finely minced	1-2	1-2
Cilantro, chopped	1 Tbsp	15 ml
Hop extract (We like Citra®)	1 tsp	5 ml
Salt and pepper		

Place about half of the avocado into a food processor with about half of the lime juice. Blitz until almost smooth.

Chop remaining avocado into small, bite sized pieces and place into a mixing bowl. Toss with remaining lime juice.

Add zest, bell pepper, onion, jalapenos, garlic, cilantro, hop extract, and pureed avocado to the mixing bowl, gently fold in until ingredients are well distributed. Season with salt and pepper to taste.

Potato Salad

Not my grandma's potato salad... well, not quite. We use a homemade vinaigrette, to which the hops bring a great amount of character. This is a more refined tasting salad.

The light bitterness works really well with the creamy texture and taste of the mayo. The hop flavour really enhances and adds a bit of something - much like using lemon zest or green onion.

Red potatoes	3-5 lbs	3000-5000g
Hopped "Italian" salad dressing (Page 110)	1 ½ cups	375 ml
Dijon mustard	1 Tbsp	15 ml
Full fat mayonnaise	3/4-1 cup	175-200 ml
Green onions, thinly sliced	3	3
Celery stalks, thinly sliced	4	4
Radishes, sliced thin	8	8
Large eggs, hard boiled and sliced	5-6	5-6
Black pepper		

Wash potatoes, chop into 3/4"-1" cubes.

Boil potato cubes until tender enough to easily pierce with a fork, but still firm – about 20-25 minutes. Strain, and place into a large non-metallic bowl.

Whisk together Hopped "Italian" dressing and Dijon mustard, pour over warm potato cubes. Gently stir to coat, cover and refrigerate overnight.

Several hours before serving, add mayonnaise into marinated potatoes - 3/4 cup if you like a drier salad, more if you like it creamier - gently stir until potatoes are evenly coated.

Add green onion, celery, and radish slices, gently fold.

Gently fold in the egg slices, season with pepper to taste.

Potato Salad

Hoppy Roasted Nuts

These nuts are addictive! The bitterness of the hops cuts the cloying sweetness of the honey, for a balanced roasted nut with a nice crunch and a ton of flavour.

These are very easy to make - just don't worry when they are soft when they first come out of the syrup, they harden as they cool.

Hop pellets work best for this recipe. Use a mortar and pestle to reduce them to a light powder before measuring.

Using 2 tsp of low acid hops are best for most people - flavour, without pain. For hopheads, you may want to use a higher acid hop, or use 3 tsp of powder. We tend to use Sterling hops for this recipe.

Makes 3 cups

Unsalted cashews	3 cups	750 ml
Granulated sugar	½ cup	125 ml
Powdered hop pellets	2 tsp	10 ml
Salt	3/4 tsp	3 ml
Liquid honey	½ cup	125 ml
Water	1/4 cup	50 ml
Olive oil	1 Tbsp	15 ml

Preheat oven to 350F (180 C), line cookie sheet with parchment paper.

Spread cashews out evenly on prepared baking sheet. Bake - stirring every 3-4 minutes or so - for about 12 minutes.

In a large bowl, combine sugar, powdered hop pellets, and salt. Set aside.

When cashews are almost finished roasting, combine honey, water and olive oil in a medium saucepan. Bring to a boil over medium-high heat, add roasted cashews and stir well to coat completely. Continue to cook, stirring constantly, until all of the liquid has absorbed, 5-6 minutes.

Pour cashews out into the large bowl, gently tossing to coat evenly with the sugar-hop mix.

Spread cashews out evenly on the still-lined baking sheet, separating them well. Allow to cool completely before storing in an airtight container.

Hoppy Roasted Nuts

Hoppy IPA Pickles

Hoppy IPA Pickles

A few years ago, I became obsessed with canning - pickle making in particular. After a bunch of playing around with some of the basics - pickles, mixed vegetable pickles, pickled carrots, etc - I got it in my head that I should do a beer pickle for my husband.

Well, after a TON of work designing the recipe – making sure the acid level was right, planning flavours to compliment the style of beer, etc – I was disappointed to learn that Dogfish Head Brewery beat me to it! Hate it when I have a great idea, only to find that someone got there first!

Anyway, these pickles are fabulous.

Also, they cost a fraction of the ready-made price AND you have the flexibility of using your favorite brew! I designed this around my husband's favorite beer – Hopslam. The hops we chose were ones we grew ourselves – Centennial – chosen because of how the flavour compliments the beer. Garlic, mustard seeds, peppercorns, and jalapenos round out the recipe, all flavours that work well with the beer.

No sugar at all, though – if you're into sweet pickles, this may not be the recipe for you. These pickles are sour, and as bitter as you want them. You can vary the level of bitterness by adjusting the amount of hops used, and the length of time you boil them in the brine. We used a full oz of "wet" hops, and boiled them for 10 minutes to produce a very bitter pickle – exactly how my husband wanted them. If you don't subscribe to his "the more bitter, the better!" mantra, feel free to use less hops, and only boil them for a few minutes.

As an idea of yield, we made a double batch of this recipe and ended up with:

- 3 quart jars (2 of whole pickles, 1 of spears)
- 4 pint jars (All as spears)
- 5 little jam jars (All as slices)

I recommend sticking to slices and spears. They look nicer, take up the flavour quicker, and require far less of the liquid. Also? The jam jars of pickle slices make really great gifts!

Pickling cucumbers, washed/scrubbed well.	2 lbs	1000 g
Vinegar (5% acidity)	5 cups	1250 ml
IPA of choice	3 cups	750 ml
Water	2 cups	500 ml
Pickling salt	½ cup	125 ml
Fresh hops	1/2-1oz	15-30 g
OR		
Dried hops	1/4 - ½ oz	7.5 - 15 g

Per pint jar (2x for quart jars):

Garlic clove, peeled and smashed	1	1
Black pepper corns	1/4 tsp	1 ml
Mustard seeds	1/4 tsp	1 ml
Jalapeno, sliced (optional)	1/4 - 1/2	1/4 - 1/2
Fresh or dried hops, optional	1-2	1-2

Canning Equipment:

LARGE pot for processing
Clean, sterilized canning jars & rings
Canning funnel
New, never-used, sterilized canning lids
Jar lifter

Slice your cucumbers into whatever form you prefer – we did spears for pint jars, and slices for little jam jars.

Fill your LARGE pot with at least 6" of water, put on medium or high heat to bring it to a boil as you prepare your brine.

In another pot (NOT the canning pot!), combine vinegar, beer, water, and salt. Bring to a boil, stirring well to dissolve the salt. Once mixture reaches a boil, add hops and stir well, mashing them around a bit. Allow them to simmer for 5-10 minutes, tasting frequently.

As your brine simmers, measure your "per jar" ingredients into your sterilized jars, along with one or two hop cones, if using. Arrange your prepared cucumbers into the jars, packing them tightly. If you'd like, cram another hop cone or two down the side – they'll want to float, so keep that in mind as you position them!

Once brine mixture has reached your desired level of bitterness, use a slotted spoon to remove all hop cones and stray hop leaves. Bring mixture to back up to a boil.

Using a canning funnel, pour boiling beer brine into prepared jars, leaving about ½" head space. Wipe off the top edges of the jar with a clean, wet towel, top each with a new, sterilized lid, and carefully screw on a clean lid ring. I like to use a kitchen towel for this, the jars are HOT! Carefully place your jars of pickles into the boiling water pot, allow to process for 15 minutes. CAREFULLY remove them, allow to cool overnight.

The next morning, check to make sure that all of the jars achieved a proper seal – try to push down in the middle of each lid. If it "pops", it did not seal. Any jars that didn't seal should be put in the fridge and used in the next few weeks.

Leave the jars alone for at least a few days, to allow the flavours to permeate the cucumbers. Store in a cool, dark area for up to 1 year, chill well before eating.

Hoppy IPA Pickles

Pickled Hop Shoots

Pickled Hop Shoots

Pickled hop shoots have been popular in Belgium for a long time, but are becoming more popular in North America lately. You can eat them right out of the jar as a snack, use as a fancy accompaniment for a cheese or relish platter, or as a pretty garnish for a Bloody Mary. There's even a place in Washington that uses them as a pizza topping!

A few notes about pickling:

1. The amount of brine you're going to need will vary widely depend on the size and amount of your shoots, the size of jar you use, and how well you pack them into the jar. Have extra vinegar on hand, and either make more brine than you think you'll need, or be prepared to make more as you go.

2. Pickling salt is usually available with the canning supplies in any grocery store. You'll want to use this, rather than regular table salt – the anti-caking additives in table salt can make your pickle brine go murky and ugly.

3. While you can use previously-used jars for canning (when WELL washed and sterilized!), you need new lids for each new batch. Safety first!

4. Pack your shoots tightly, but gently - try not to break them! Just know that no matter how tightly you think you've packed them, they'll probably float!

Fresh hop shoots	1 lb	1000g

Brine:

Vinegar	4 cups	1000 ml
Water	4 cups	1000 ml
Pickling salt	1/3 cup	75 ml

Per pint jar (2x for quart jars):

Dill seed	½ - 1 tsp	2-5 ml
Garlic cloves, peeled and cut in half	1-2	1-2
Black peppercorns	1/4 tsp	1 ml
Mustard seed	1/4 tsp	1 ml
Jalapeno slices (optional)		
Fresh or dried hops (optional)	2-3	2-3

Canning Equipment:

LARGE pot for processing
Clean, sterilized canning jars & rings
New, never-used, sterilized canning lids
Canning funnel
Jar lifter (nice to have, not necessary if you can handle pain!)

Wash and trim shoots - you can leave some small leaves on, if you'd like.

Fill your LARGE pot with at least 6" of water, put on medium or high heat to bring it to a boil as you prepare your brine.

In another pot (NOT the canning pot!), combine vinegar, water, and pickling salt. Bring to a boil, stirring well to dissolve the salt. As the brine heats up, measure your "per jar" ingredients into your sterilized jars. Arrange your prepared hop shoots into the jars, packing them tightly – seriously, try to cram as many shoots into each jar as you can!

Once brine comes to a boil, use a canning funnel to pour brine into prepared jars, leaving about 1/2" head space. Wipe off the top edges of the jar with a clean, wet towel, top each with a new, sterilized lid, and carefully screw on a clean lid ring. I like to use a kitchen towel for this, the jars are HOT! Carefully place your jars of pickles into the boiling water pot, allow to process for 15 minutes. CAREFULLY remove them, allow to cool overnight.

The next morning, check to make sure that all of the jars achieved a proper seal – try to push down in the middle of each lid. If it "pops", it did not seal. Any jars that didn't seal should be put in the fridge and used in the next few weeks.

Leave the jars alone for at least a few days, to allow the flavours to permeate the hop shoots. Store in a cool, dark area (ideally) for up to 1 year, chill well before eating.

Freshly canned, and after five minutes. Big change in colour!

Grilled Cheese Stuffed Hop Leaves

Sometimes, the recipe that ends up in the cookbook is a long way off from the idea it started as. This one happens to be a great example of that.

This recipe started off as an idea for making cheese stuffed hop leaves. They would have been stuffed with cream cheese and cheddar, and sauteed - much the way that rice stuffed hop leaves are done. One thing led to another, and they ended up filled with goat cheese, kalamata olives, a little chopped pepperoncini, and fresh herbs, before being grilled!

THESE resulted in one of those deep eye contact, gooey declarations of "I love you" from my husband that I tend to think of being usually reserved for like.. weddings and probably child births. I don't know.. Bottom line: they were *fantastic*!

Hop leaves	30	30
Goat cheese	8 oz	250 g
Garlic cloves, pressed or finely minced	3-4	3-4
Pitted kalamata olives	1/4 cup	50 ml
Pepperoncini	2-3	2-3
Fresh oregano	1 tsp	5 ml
Salt and Pepper		
Olive oil		

Heat your grill up. We like to use charcoal for this, but gas grills will work as well.

Rinse hop leaves, cut stems off right at the edge of each leaf, discard stems. Place into a large pot of boiling water and cook for two minutes. Transfer to a large bowl of cold water, set aside.

Place goat cheese in a small mixing bowl, beat until smooth. Mince or press the garlic, and finely chop olives, pepperoncini, and oregano. Add minced/chopped ingredients to the cheese, stirring until well distributed. Season with salt and pepper, to taste.

Drain leaves from cold water. Arrange leaves on a clean work surface, smooth side down / veiny side up. Place 1 Tbsp of filling in the center of each leaf, right above where the stem was.

Fold bottom section of leaves up over filling, pressing lightly to secure. Fold sides in over filling, then roll leaf/filing over itself a couple of times to completely encapsulate the filling. Repeat with remaining leaves, until all of the filling is used up.

Brush each packet with olive oil, grill over direct heat for about 1 minute. Use two forks to carefully flip them, grill for another minute or so on the second side. Serve hot!

Filling Variations:

Herbed Goat & Feta:

Goat cheese	8 oz	250 g
Feta cheese	2 oz	55 g
Garlic cloves, pressed or finely minced	3-4	3-4
Fresh dill	1/4 cup	50 ml
Fresh mint	2 Tbsp	30 ml
Fresh oregano	1 tsp	5 ml
Lemon zest	1 tsp	5 ml
Salt and Pepper		

Beat goat and feta cheeses until smooth. Mince or press garlic, finely chop dill, mint, and oregano. Add garlic, herbs, and lemon zest to cheese mixture, stir until well combined. Season with salt and pepper to taste.

Jalapeno Popper:

Cream cheese	8 oz	250g
Shredded sharp cheddar cheese	4 oz	125g
Jalapeno peppers	1-2	1-2
Salt and Pepper		

Beat cream cheese until smooth. Add cheddar cheese, mix until well combined.

Seed and finely chop jalapenos, add to cheese mixture and mix well. Season with salt and pepper to taste.

Grilled Cheese Stuffed Hop Leaves

Mediterranean Style Stuffed Hop Leaves

Mediterranean Style Stuffed Hop Leaves

Porter is a big fan of stuffed grape leaves in general, but the canned version at the store always look so .. off. With a ton of fresh hop leaves on hand, we knew what we had to do!

The use of fresh herbs and lemon give this a brightness that he loved. Also stated that the difference between these and normal canned grape leaves are like comparing fresh spring rolls to egg rolls. I get it. It's a bright, happy spring taste. The freshness of everything really comes through.

The leaves themselves have a great texture . He compares it to sushi - the slightly soggy texture of an older roll, vs the crispness of freshly made sushi - he sees that as the difference between canned grape leaves, and fresh hop leaves - The hop leaves being more like fresh sushi.

Makes about 30

Olive oil	2 Tbsp	30 ml
Small onion, chopped	1	1
Garlic cloves, pressed or finely minced	2-3	2-3
Uncooked rice	1 cup	250 ml
Chicken broth	2 cups	500 ml
Lemon, zest of	1	1
Green onions, finely chopped	2	2
Fresh dill, chopped	1/3 cup	75 ml
Fresh mint, chopped	2 Tbsp	30 ml
Salt and pepper		
Fresh hop leaves	~30	~30
Olive oil	2 Tbsp	30 ml

In a medium saucepan, saute onion in olive oil until translucent. Add garlic, continue cooking for 1 minute. Add rice and chicken broth, cover and cook over medium heat for 15 minutes.

After 15 minutes, add lemon zest, green onion, dill and mint. Stir well, season with salt and pepper to taste. Remove from heat, set aside.

Rinse hop leaves, cut stems off right at the edge of each leaf, discard stems. Place into a large pot of boiling water and cook for two minutes. Transfer to a large bowl of cold water, allow to sit for 1 minute before draining.

Arrange leaves on a clean work surface, smooth side down / veiny side up. Place 1 generous teaspoon of filling in the center of each leaf, right above where the stem was

Fold bottom section of leaves up over filling, pressing lightly to secure.

Fold sides in over filling, then roll leaf/filing over itself a couple of times to tightly encapsulate the filling. Repeat with remaining leaves, until all of the filling is used up.

Spread olive oil over bottom of a medium saucepan, cover with a few hop leaves. Arrange stuffed hop leaves in the saucepan, seam side down.

Add just enough water to cover the stuffed leaf rolls. Cover with a plate that just fits within the pan, to keep rolls submerged.

Bring water to a boil, turn heat down and hold at a simmer for about 15 minutes. Remove from heat, gently transfer rolls to a plate.

Rolls can be served hot, cold, or room temperature.

Hopped Mozzarella

Fresh mozzarella is usually a semi-spontaneous treat in our house. We'll be doing our groceries, and pick up a gallon of whole milk to make a batch, usually within a day or two.

Having made it so many times, it only takes me about 15-17 minutes from the time I take the milk out of the fridge, to cutting into a warm ball of fresh cheese. It's quick, easy, and doesn't take much in terms of ingredients.

When writing this book, we decided to see if we could do a hopped mozzarella. We did, and it was great! The hops added an elegance to the flavour, You'd never pick it out as "hops", it just tasted more... refined. As if we'd used really fresh, expensive milk - there was a bright, almost grassy flavour to it. You'd never pinpoint it as hops - it's subtle on its own, but if you were to make it with and without, it would be really obvious that SOMETHING is different. It really elevates just basic grocery store milk cheese to something sublime.

If you'd like more "in your face" hops flavour, feel free to increase the amount used.

In addition to hop pellets, you will need rennet and citric acid, which are available at specialty cooking stores, or home brewing / cheese making supply shops.

Makes about 1 lb of cheese

Ingredient	Imperial	Metric
Unchlorinated water, divided (spring water)	1 - 1 1/4 cups	250 - 300 ml
Hop pellets	1 Tbsp	15 ml
Lipase, optional*	1/4 tsp	1 ml
Fresh milk – NOT "ultra pasteurized"	1 Gallon	4 L
Citric acid	1 ½ tsp	7 ml
Liquid rennet (or 1/4 rennet tablet, crushed)	1/4 tsp	1 ml
Cheese salt (or fine salt)	1 tsp	5 ml

Heat 1/2 cup of water to a simmer, add hop pellets and allow to steep for 5 minutes. Strain through fine cheesecloth - pressing gently - discard solids.

If using lipase, dissolve it in 1/4 cup water, allow to sit for 15 minutes.

Pour milk and hop water into a large, very clean pan. Heat over medium, until it reaches 55F (13C)

While the milk is heating, dissolve citric acid in 1/4 cup of water, and rennet in another 1/4 cup of water. Keep the two (or three, if using lipase!) solutions straight – label if you have to!

Once cheese reaches 55F (13C), stir in the citric acid solution. The milk will start to curdle a little.

Add lipase – if using – and stir well. Continue to heat milk, stirring often.

Continue heating to 88F (31C). When milk comes to 88F (31C), add rennet solution and stir VERY well – be sure to use some up and down motions as well as "around", to distribute the rennet.

Continue to heat to 105F (41C), stirring gently. The curds will separate from the whey.

Between 100 and 105F (38-41C), the liquid will no longer look milky – instead it will be clear and yellowish. When this happens, you're ready for the next step!

Using a slotted spoon, carefully remove all of the curds from the whey, transferring it to a microwave safe bowl. Once all of the curd is transferred, press with a spoon to force out excess whey. Drain any whey visible in the bowl.

Microwave the curd for about a minute on high. If you don't have a high pain tolerance, clean rubber gloves will come in handy for this next step.

GENTLY fold the curd over itself a few times, trying not to burn yourself. The idea is to distribute the heat, NOT to beat the life out of it.

Microwave for another 30 seconds, drain whey, fold over a few more times. Repeat one more time, and add salt if you're using it.

By this time, the cheese should be hot enough to stretch. Stretch and fold a few times – as if you were stretching taffy – until the cheese is smooth and shiny.

Once you've determined that either your cheese is smooth/shiny enough, or you're just hungry and tired of burning your hands… do with it as you please:

- Pinch it into small balls

- Roll it in a log

- Roll three logs and braid them.

- Make a large ball, as pictured.

We like to serve our fresh cheese right away, when it's warm and squeaky!

Hopped Fresh Mozzarella

Smoked Hop Leaves

Smoked hop leaves are fun and easy to make - my husband always loves any excuse to put something in the smoker - and make a great, healthy alternative to potato chips.

These have a really satisfying crunch to them, with a salty bite. The smoke adds a complex, umami taste, while the oil and salt satisfies that potato chip craving.

Because the leaves really take up the flavour of the smoke well, you have a ton of potential for flavours, based on the types of wood chips available.

Hop leaves, stems removed
Olive oil
Salt

Rinse and pat dry your hop leaves. In a large bowl, toss your hop leaves with a little olive oil - just enough to lightly coat them. Sprinkle with salt.

Arrange prepared leaves in a single layer on your smoking racks, hot smoke at around 225 F (107 C) for about 15 minutes. Leaves are ready when they are dry and crispy.

Oven Hop Leaf Chips

Don't have a smoker? No problem - you can make Hop leaf chips in the oven, too!

Hop leaves, stems removed
Olive oil spray
Salt

Preheat oven to 350 F (180 C)

Line several cookie sheets with parchment paper, spray with olive oil.

Rinse and pat dry your hop leaves. Arrange leaves on cookie sheets, so that they are tightly spaced, but not overlapping. Spray olive oil across the tops, then sprinkle with a little salt.

Bake hop leaves 1 sheet at a time for 10-12 minutes, or until completely dry. Cool a little, then enjoy!

These are great fresh out of the oven, but can also be put aside for later – IF they last!

Smoked Hop Leaves

Hop Leaf Smoked Cheeses

Hop leaf smoked cheeses are a little bit of work - easy to do, but with a few steps involved and it needs to be planned in advance. It's well worth the effort though - each step brings something else to the table, or aids the process overall.

Pre-smoking the leaves infuses them with flavour, while soaking them adds more flavour, changes the texture, and has the moisture act as a carrier for the smoke flavour. In the end, the result is a gorgeous, elegant cheese presentation.

You can do this with any kind of cheese you want - our favourites are gouda and goat cheese. (Smoked goat cheese is LIFE!)

Several large hop leaves
Wine or spirit of choice - we like bourbon for this.
Cheese of choice

Cold smoke large hop leaves for 4-5 hours, or until fairly dry.

Place smoked leaves in an container that has a lid. Cover with wine or spirit of choice, tightly seal, and chill for a week or two, until leaves are well infused and pliable.

Cold smoke cheese of choice for 1-3 hours. Wrap smoked cheese in soaked hop leaves, tightly wrap in plastic wrap to mold leaves to cheese, chill 20 minutes.

Cold smoke for another 2 hours. Chill before serving.

To really get the maximum benefit from the use of leaves, you'll want to wrap them up and let them age for a week or two in your fridge... but we tend to inhale them as soon as they're cool!

Hop Leaf Smoked Cheeses

Hopcorn Seasoning

We love creating popcorn seasonings for our own home use. Everything from nacho cheese to ketchup and all-dressed, it's fun to experiment with our own unique blends.

We thought it would be fun to use the base flavours in beer to create a fun new popcorn seasoning - well, hopcorn seasoning!

In addition to the hops, we used dry malt extract - a sweet flavour - as well as nutritional yeast for an added flavour boost, and to balance the sweetness of the malt. The hops and salt balance it all out, creating a mix that is mildly reminiscent of beer, without being super intense or overwhelming.

Friends of ours who can't stand beer love this, and beer lovers also adore it. The sweet/salty mix is perfect for popcorn.

Says one friend:

"This popcorn you left at my place! I have to say, I dislike beer. I've tried, several times, to come around to beer, and I always have trouble drinking it. That said, I am eating this popcorn by the fist full. It definitely still has a lot of the same flavour profile that has pushed me away from beer, but it's not overwhelming. I think that things like this could be what help me adjust to the hoppy taste and ultimately come around to beer. Maybe. One day."

I'll take it!

As written here, this is a great, balanced popcorn seasoning. If you're more of a "More bitter, the better!" hophead like my husband, you can add another 1-2 tsp hop powder

Makes about 1 cup of seasoning

Dry malt extract (DME)	½ cup	125 ml
Nutritional yeast flakes	1/4 cup	50 ml
Hop Powder (Low acid variety!)	4 tsp	20 ml
Salt	4 tsp	20 ml

Combine ingredients, distributing everything well. You can do this by hand, or in a small food processor or spice grinder, for a finer texture

Store in an airtight shaker container.

To serve, shake a little over hot buttered popcorn

Hopcorn Seasoning

Beer and Broccoli Soup

Main Dishes

Beer and Broccoli Soup

Not just cheesy broccoli, this is a complex, elegant soup. The crunch of the celery - if you don't overcook it - really adds some texture and interest to the dish. The hops give it a little bit of attitude without being overwhelming.

This soup can be made thicker if you like. It's well balanced as an actual soup, not just as a thinned out fondue. The hops leaves add fun little bursts of hop flavour to this soup - we use frequently Cascade hops for this.

Makes 6-8 servings

Olive oil	2 Tbsp	30 ml
Celery stalks, thinly sliced	2	2
Medium onion, chopped	1	1
Large carrots, grated	2	2
Broccoli florets	2 cups	500 ml
Garlic cloves, pressed or finely minced	3	3
Salt and pepper		
Butter	1/4 cup	50 ml
Flour- wheat or rice	1/4 cup	50 ml
Dijon mustard	2 Tbsp	30 ml
Chicken broth	3 cups	750 ml
IPA beer of choice	1 ½ cups	375 ml
Milk	3 cups	750 ml
Shredded sharp Cheddar cheese	6 cups	1500 ml
Shredded Parmesan cheese	1/4 cup	50 ml
Dried hop leaves, crushed	2 Tbsp	30 ml

In a large pot, combine olive oil, celery, and onion. Cook over medium heat until onions begin to soften. Add carrots, broccoli, and garlic, sprinkle with a little salt and pepper, and cook until vegetables are fairly tender.

Add butter, stir until melted. Sprinkle flour over the vegetable and butter mixture, gently stir to combine. Cook - stirring frequently - for 2 minutes.

Once 2 minutes have passed, add Dijon mustard and whisk to combine before adding chicken broth, beer, and milk. Bring soup just up to a simmer, and hops and stir well. Add cheeses and cook, stirring constantly, until cheeses are melted and soup is smooth. Serve hot.

Hoppy Citrus IPA Glazed Wings

These wings were one of the first hop recipes I designed, for one of our hop harvests.

I've said it before… I'm not a fan of drinking beer, but I do LOVE it as an ingredient. In these wings? Completely fantastic! The flavours went together so well, complex but coherent, and definitely unique. It was sweet and savoury with a little heat and a little bit of bitter hop bite – perfectly balanced, and so, SO good. Let me share what the hop heads had to say about it, though:

"Hop wings! These little treats were covered lightly in a light orange glaze, and they looked really good. My first bite was a great crisp feel followed by first a nice honey taste, followed with the fresh taste of citrus from an orange, it was then all combined at the end with the bitterness from the hop. Very much like a very good beer the taste had the distinct front, middle and end tastes you would expect. It was truly delicious!" – Trevor

"These hop wings are delicious! The flavours explode in your mouth, with sweet honey and orange popping up first and the slightly bitter citrus finish with a little bit of spice. I tore through my wings super fast, this is an addictive sauce! It's not simply a variation of another sauce or a replication of a commercial sauce, this stands out on its own so well. I love trying new flavours of wings, but this is one where I'd keep coming back to it over and over, it quickly became my favorite." – Porter

An interesting note about my husband: He has some weird "top of the food chain guilt" thing going on. He doesn't mind eating meat, he just doesn't want to be reminded that it used to be an animal… so he hates eating food off the bone. I think this is the first time I've seen him seem totally OK with eating non-boneless wings!

A note about hops: While we used fresh hops – Centennial, as that's what we had readily available – you can also use dried. Use about half as much, if you're going with dried.

Vegetable Oil for deep frying		
Fresh chicken wings	4 lbs	2 kg
Salt		
IPA of choice	1 cup	250 ml
Fresh hops, divided	½ cup	125 ml
Liquid honey	1 cup	250 ml
Jalapeno pepper, finely chopped	1	1
Garlic cloves, pressed or finely minced	2	2
Orange, Juice and zest of	1	1

Heat oil 375 F (190 C). You can use a deep fryer, or a heavy pan. If not using a deep fryer, use a deep, heavy pot, filled to at least 3" deep. Sprinkle chicken generously with salt, allow to air dry while preparing glaze.

In a medium saucepan, bring IPA and 1/4 cup of the hops to a boil. Turn heat down to medium-low, simmer until it has reduce to about half the original volume. (Just eyeball it!).

Once IPA has reduced, add honey, jalapeno, garlic cloves, orange zest/juice, and a pinch of salt. Bring back up to a simmer, simmer for about 10 minutes. Add remaining hops, simmer for 5 more minutes. Pour glaze through wire strainer, discarding solids left behind. Return to pot and keep warm while preparing chicken wings.

Fry chicken wings in batches of about a dozen pieces each – allowing oil to come back up to temperature between each batch – until golden brown. (About 10-15 minutes per batch). Transfer fried wings to a large bowl, toss with glaze, and serve hot!

Hoppy Citrus IPA Glazed Wings
67

Hop Leaf Wreath

Hop Leaf Wreath

Ever hear of "Lazy Cabbage Rolls"? It's a recipe we used to make back home when we wanted cabbage rolls, but were...well, feeling lazy about it. Just layers of cabbage and rice, no bothering to roll them up.

This is a lot like that, hitting on many of the same flavours incorporated in a traditional stuffed leaf recipe. Goat and feta cheeses are added not only for flavour and texture, but to hold the mixture together as a sliceable loaf for serving.

This dish ended up having the after-eating properties of a well loved comfort food, where you kind of have to lean back, put your feet up, and bask in that "fat and happy feeling" ... which was kind of amazing, given how HEALTHY it was. Very hearty meal, though!

Jasmine rice	1 cup	250 ml
Chicken broth or stock, divided	2 cups	500 ml
Large hop leaves	30- 40	30-40
Olive oil	2 Tbsp	30 ml
Large onion, chopped	1	1
Garlic cloves, pressed or finely minced	4	4
Ground lamb or pork	2 lbs	1 Kg
Lemon, zest and juice of	1	1
Fresh dill, chopped	1 cup	250 ml
Fresh mint, finely chopped	2 Tbsp	30 ml
Goat cheese	12 oz	350 g
Feta cheese	4 oz	125 g
Nutmeg	1/4 tsp	1 ml
Salt and pepper, to taste		
Olive oil		

Preheat oven to 375F (190 C), prepare rice with 1 cup of the stock/broth. Fluff, set aside.

Rinse hop leaves, cut stems off right at the edge of each leaf, discard stems. Place into a large pot of boiling water and cook for two minutes. Transfer to a large bowl of cold water, set aside.

In a large pan, cook onion and garlic in olive oil, until onions start to soften. Add ground meat, cook until browned. Add prepared rice, 1/2 cup of the remaining broth/stock, and lemon zest and juice. Stir well, cook for one minute. Remove from heat.

Add dill, mint, cheeses, and nutmeg to pan, stir well to combine. Season with salt and pepper to taste, set aside.

Brush Bundt or ring pan liberally with olive oil. Arrange some hop leaves in the pan as a single layer - smooth side down, veiny side up - each leaf slightly overlapping the leaves around it. Extend the leaves up over the edges of the pan, both around the outside, and around the inner ring. Repeat for 2 more layers, overlapping previous layers.

Carefully spoon filling into the pan, gently packing into the crevices of the pan. Once all the filling is in the pan, use the back of a spoon to smooth the surface of the filling. Fold down the hop leaves that extended past the end of the pan to completely cover the filling. If the leaves don't completely cover the filling, add some more leaves to the top, pressing gently against the filling.

Pour remaining ½ cup of broth/stock over the leaves, cover pan with foil, and bake for 35 minutes. Allow pan to cool for 5 minutes before inverting onto serving dish. Serve hot.

Marinated Chicken and Vegetable Skewers

Over the years, we have marinated a lot of chicken. Commercially available marinades, homemade marinades... whether thrown together or planned out.

... this is probably the best chicken marinade that either of us has ever had. Perfectly balanced flavours, oil vs acid... works great on chicken, veggies, pork, and even fish/seafood. We could live on this one!

We tend to use powdered hop pellets for this - usually Amarillo® - but you can also use 1 tsp of dried hops that have been blitzed in a spice grinder.

Chicken breasts	3	3
Button mushrooms	8 oz	250 g
Zucchini	1-2	1-2
Olive oil	1/3 cup	75 ml
Cider vinegar	½ cup	125 ml
Light brown sugar, packed	1/4 cup	50 ml
Dijon mustard	2 Tbsp	30 ml
Garlic cloves, pressed or finely minced	4	4
Pellet hops powder	½ tsp	2 ml
Salt & pepper		

Trim chicken breasts, cut into 1" cubes. Wash mushrooms and zucchini, slice zucchini into ½" thick slices. Place prepared chicken and vegetables into a non-metallic bowl or dish (with a lid).

Whisk together all remaining ingredients, aside from salt and pepper. Season with salt and pepper to taste. Pour over chicken and vegetables, stir well to coat. Chill for 1 hour.

Thread chicken onto skewers, and vegetables onto separate skewers (they'll have different cook times). Grill until chicken is cooked through, and vegetables are as cooked as you like them.

Serve hot.

Marinated Chicken and Vegetable Skewers

Jerk Chicken

Ok, I'll admit - there are a few ways that this recipe diverges from traditional Jerk chicken... mostly for convenience / availability of ingredients.

For instance, Scotch bonnet peppers are traditional, but I can never find them around here! Habaneros are a reasonable substitution. Additionally, traditional Jerk is cooked over a set up of pimento leaves and wood, but those are also very difficult to find for most people. If you have them, great - use them! If not, just grill these as you would any other chicken recipe.

At 4 habanero pepperss, you get a fair bit of heat, but nothing my Minnesotan husband couldn't (happily!) handle. It's not quite hot enough to be a proper jerk chicken, but it has the absolute best balance of flavours. For more heat, boost it up to 6 habaneros.

Be sure to use a hop with ton of flavour, so it adds to the mix, rather than get drowned out by it. Peppery, earthy, and citrus hops work best in this recipe. I love Citra ® hops for this - the flavour of the hops really rounds out the flavour mix of the rest of the ingredients. If you'd like to use pellet hops for this, grind them into a powder and use about 2 tsp, or to taste

Small red onion	1	1
Green onions	3	3
Garlic cloves, pressed or finely minced	8	8
Habanero peppers	4-6	4-6
Brown sugar, packed	1/4 cup	50 ml
Fresh ginger, minced or pureed	2 Tbsp	30 ml
Fresh thyme leaves	2 Tbsp	30 ml
Allspice	1 Tbsp	15 ml
Coarse ground black pepper	2 tsp	10 ml
Nutmeg	1 tsp	5 ml
Cinnamon	1 tsp	5 ml
Salt	1 tsp	5 ml
Ground cloves	½ tsp	2 ml
Soy sauce	½ cup	125 ml
Orange juice	½ cup	125 ml
Vinegar	½ cup	125 ml
Olive oil	1/4 cup	50 ml
Lime, juice of	1	1
Dried hop leaves	1/4 cup	50 ml
Chicken, broken down into pieces	1 large	1 large

Rough chop onion, green onions, garlic, and habaneros, add to a blender or food processor with all other ingredients EXCEPT chicken. Blitz until well processed and smooth.

Marinate chicken in jerk sauce overnight.

Remove chicken from sauce, grill until done.

Jerk Chicken

Pasta Primavera

Pasta primavera is all about contrasts - contrast in texture between the noodles and crunchy vegetables. Contrast in mouthfeel between the bright freshness of those vegetables, and the richness of a butter, cream, and cheese based sauce. Also, visual contrast when it comes to the colours of the vegetables, and those of the pasta and sauce.

This dish was one of the first that I wanted to make, when we decided to create this cookbook. I love vegetables, and was craving a big mess of them something fierce at the time. I thought it would be great to add a little bit of bitter right into the sauce, contrasting with smooth, heaviness of it. We chose to use Pacific Jade hops, for bringing not only a bright citrussy flavour to the sauce, but also crushed black pepper aroma. I'd recommend using a citrussy or spicy hop with this dish.

Serves 4-6

Butter	2 Tbsp	30 ml
Corn starch	2 tsp	10 ml
Garlic cloves, pressed or finely minced	2	2
Granulated sugar	1 Tbsp	15 ml
Baking soda	1/2 tsp	2 ml
Heavy cream	2 cups	500 ml
Grated Asiago or Parmesan cheese	1/2 cup	125 ml
Fresh basil leaves, chiffonade	1-2 Tbsp	15-30 ml
Finely ground hop pellets	1/2 tsp	2 ml
Salt and pepper		
Dry pasta, like penne	1 lb	500 g
Olive Oil	1 Tbsp	15 ml

White onion, thinly sliced	1	1
Garlic cloves, pressed or finely minced	2	2
Small broccoli florets	1 ½ cups	375 ml
White mushrooms, sliced	4 oz	125 g
Zucchini, sliced	1 medium	1 medium
Asparagus spears, sliced diagonally	8	8
Green bell pepper, sliced	½	½
Green pea pods	½ - 1 cup	125-250 ml

OR

Red onion, sliced	½	½
Small/medium yellow squash	1	1
White mushrooms, sliced	4 oz	125 g
Small broccoli florets	1 cup	250 ml
Green pea pods	1 cup	250 ml
Green onion, thinly sliced	1	1
Carrots, thinly sliced	2	2
Red bell pepper, sliced	1	1

In a medium sauce pan, melt butter. Add cornstarch, whisk until smooth. Add garlic, sugar, and baking soda, whisk until well combined. Add heavy cream, bring JUST to a boil. Add cheese, continue stirring until melted and smooth.

Add basil and hop powder, reduce heat to low. Season with salt and pepper to taste.

In a large pot, bring water to a boil. Cook pasta per directions. While pasta is cooking, prepare vegetables:

In a large fry pan or wok, saute onion and garlic in olive oil until onion goes translucent. Add rest of vegetables, saute JUST until warm. You don't want them to actually cook through or go soft.

Strain pasta, gently toss with sauce and vegetables, serve immediately.

Pasta Primavera

Baked Chicken Coating

This coating makes for a chicken dish with delicious crunch and complex flavour. We like a low acid, earthy hop for this - like Saaz.

The earthy, peppery, and lemony tones incorporated into this coating really pop, and work perfectly with the chicken. Corn flakes, elevated! You can mix the dry ingredients and store them until you're ready to use them, or make the dish from start to finish.

Mayo makes the chicken even more tender and juicy, but can be swapped out for milk. If using milk, dip the chicken pieces, rather than brush them.

A note on smoked serrano powder: You may have to order this online, as it's not typically found in grocery stores. SO worth the cost and effort - it packs a flavour and heat that brings so much to anything you use it on. However, if you need to forgo that for any reason, you can substitute smoked paprika.

Serves 4

Corn flake crumbs	1 cup	250 ml
Salt	1/2 tsp +	2 ml +
Coarse ground black pepper	1/2 tsp +	2 ml +
Finely powdered hop pellets	1/2 tsp	2 ml
Smoked serrano powder	1/4 tsp	1 ml
Garlic powder	1/4 tsp	1 ml
Onion powder	Pinch	Pinch
Butter, melted	2 Tbsp	30 ml
Mayonnaise	1/4 cup	50 ml
Boneless skinless chicken breasts	4	4

Preheat oven to 375 F (190 C)

Combine corn flakes, salt, pepper, powdered hops, and serrano, garlic, and onion powders, stirring until well combined. Add melted butter, stir just to coat crumbs. Taste, adjust salt and pepper if desired.

Lightly season chicken breasts with a little more salt and pepper. Brush individual chicken breasts with the mayo, then roll in the crumbs mixture. Transfer to a parchment lined baking sheet.

Bake for about 45 minutes, or until golden, and juices run clear when poked / cut.

Baked Chicken Coating

77

Hearty Beef Stew

This stew tastes like something you'd get at a really nice pub. The beer works so well with the beef and root vegetables, and the hops brighten the whole thing up. Use an earthy hop for this.

Makes about 28 cups

Stewing beef, cut up into chunks	4 lbs	2 Kg
Vegetable oil	2 Tbsp	30 ml
Large onion, chopped	1	1
Beef broth	12 cups	3 L
Dry red wine	3 cups	750 ml
Ribs celery	4-6	4-5
Dried savoury	1 Tbsp +	15 ml +
Black pepper	1 Tbsp +	15 ml +
Salt		
Rutabaga, peeled and chopped	1	1
Parsnips, peeled, sliced into large chunks	5	5
Carrots, peeled, sliced into chunks	6	6
Mushrooms, cut in large chunks	1 ½ lbs	750 g
Red potatoes, cut into large chunks	3-4 lbs	1 ½-2 Kg
Fresh Brussels sprouts, halved	2-3 lbs	1- 1 ½ Kg
Garlic cloves, pressed or finely minced	5	5
Vegetable oil	2 Tbsp	30 ml
Butter	3/4 cup	150 ml
Flour or rice flour	1 cup	250 ml
Dried Fuggle leaves, blitzed	1/4 cup	50 ml

In a very large, heavy pot, brown meat in oil. Add onions, continue to cook until translucent. Add beef broth, red wine, 1 rib celery, 1 Tbsp each of dried savoury and black pepper, and 2 tsp salt. Bring up to almost a boil, reduce heat and simmer – covered – for two hours.

Remove celery rib from the stew, discard. Chop remaining celery, add to pot along with rutabaga, parsnips, carrots, and mushrooms, continue simmering for another hour. Add potatoes and Brussels sprouts. Cover and simmer for another hour or so. While the stew simmers, prepare your roux:

In a large heavy pot, combine vegetable oil and butter. Heat over medium until the butter melts, stir in the flour. Without leaving your stove (Seriously!), stir the mixture constantly over medium heat until it gets quite dark – I like to get it to a reddish brown colour. It'll take time, but it's worth it – this great flavour to the stew … just don't burn it!

Stir a ladle worth of stew stock into the roux – it'll boil up and steam, don't worry. Whisk it till smooth, then add another ladle worth of stew liquid. Continue until you have a decent amount of smooth gravy. Add the gravy into the stew, stirring well to fully distribute. Stir in dried hop leaves, season with salt, pepper, and additional savoury to taste.

Hearty Beef Stew

Sweet and Sour chicken

This is a delicious take on a relatively traditional dish - the ginger, hops - we used Cascade - and sweetness make the whole thing glow - Porter says he could live on this.

Oil for deep frying – we used vegetable oil		
Garbanzo flour	1 1/4 cup	300 ml
White rice flour	1/4 cup	50 ml
Baking powder	1/4 tsp	1 ml
Salt	1 tsp	5 ml
Vegetable oil	1 tsp	5 ml
Water	1 cup	250 ml
Red bell pepper	1	1
Green bell pepper	1	1
Red onion	½	1/2
Olive oil	2 Tbsp	30 ml
Can pineapple chunks	20 oz	567 g
Brown sugar, packed	1/3 cup	75 ml
Cornstarch	1 Tbsp	15 ml
Rice wine vinegar	1/4 cup	50 ml
Freshly grated ginger	1 Tbsp	15 ml
Garlic cloves, pressed or finely minced	2-3	2-3
Salt and pepper		
Dry hop leaves, crushed	1 Tbsp	15 ml
Chicken breasts, trimmed, cut into chunks	3	3
Additional garbanzo bean flour	1/4 cup	50 ml

Start heating your oil to 375F (190 C) – you'll want at least 2-3"of oil in your pot or deep fryer.

In a large bowl, combine flours, baking powder, salt, and vegetable oil. Add water, stir well to form a thick batter. All batter to sit for 5 minutes or so, to soften the bean flour.

Chop peppers and onion into large pieces (1"), add to a large saucepan along with olive oil. Cook over medium heat until peppers just start to soften. Drain pineapples, reserving juice. Add pineapple chunks to the pot.

In a separate bowl, combine ½ cup of reserved pineapple juice, along with next ingredients up to and including garlic. Whisk until smooth with NO lumps of cornstarch. Add mixture to pot, bring just to a boil, then turn temperature down to low. Add hops, season with salt and pepper to taste, set aside while you fry the chicken.

Toss chicken chunks with additional garbanzo flour, then dredge in the batter. Carefully transfer a few battered chicken pieces to the preheated oil. Fry for a few minutes on each side, until golden brown and cooked all the way through. Use a slotted metal spoon to transfer fried chicken to paper towels.

Once all chicken is fried, toss with Sweet & Sour sauce, serve immediately.

Sweet and Sour Chicken

Bacon, Beer, & Hop Shoot Mussels

I love mussels! When I lived on the coast, I used to cook big batches of them over outdoor fires - just the mussels, water, and a little salt. Sometimes, we'd get fancy and steam them in beer.

Beer and mussels go great together. Mussels and hop shoots go great together. Bacon goes well with basically everything... so I combined them all in this recipe. Definitely a few steps up from my old backyard cookouts!

If you haven't purchased mussels before, there are a few things you should know:

Ideally, buy your mussels the same day you plan to use them, always from a reputable seller. Take a whiff - they should smell fresh, not fishy.

Mussels are a live product, and may be in various stages of closed/mostly closed/peeking open, etc when you buy them and start to prepare them. Any that aren't totally closed by the time you go to cook them, throw out.

Rinse mussels in a strainer under cold running water, shaking gently.

Mussels may have their "beards" sticking out of their shells - gently pull to remove. If you encounter any stubborn ones, trim with kitchen scissors.

After de-bearding, rinse once again by shaking under cold running water. Check for any opened mussels at this time, and discard.

Serves 2 as a main course, or 4 as an appetizer

Thick cut bacon slices , chopped	6	6
Small shallots, thinly sliced	2	2
Beer of choice	1 ½ cups	375 ml
Butter	2 Tbsp	30 ml
Salt	1/4-1/2 tsp	1-2 ml
Pepper	1 tsp	5 ml
Fresh mussels	2 lbs	1 kg
Trimmed hop shoots	2 cups	500 ml

In a large pot over medium-high heat, saute bacon, until desired level of crispiness. Add shallots, continue cooking until tender.

Add beer and butter. Stir well, season with salt and pepper to taste. Bring just to a boil.

Add mussels and hop shoots, cover. Cook for 3 minutes, check for doneness. If the majority of mussels haven't opened up wide, cover and steam for another 2 minutes.

Discard any mussels that haven't opened up, serve immediately.

Bacon, Beer, & Hop Shoot Mussels

Chili Verde

Chili Verde

A few years ago, my husband and I worked together to develop a chili recipe together, for a contest at work. His big mission, as he put it, was to "show the world that tomatoes suck".

Yeah, he's one of those people. "I feel that tomatoes should be handled like smallpox, and eradicated from the earth in the same manner" is a direct quote.

So, we decided to do a chili verde, swapping out the tomatoes in favour of tomatillos, which he does tolerate. Chili verde isn't much of a thing here in Minnesota - and really wasn't much of a thing back home in Canada, either - so we decided to make it our own.

I'm firmly in the "chili must have beans" camp, so it does. Also, while pork butt/shoulder is traditional... I find it to be a pain to cut up and trim the fat from, so I used a boneless tenderloin roast.

Both of us are in the "a little spice, but tons of flavour" camp. I'm not a fan of chili where "hot" *is* the flavour. We didn't aim for a lot of heat, instead bringing out a ton of flavours by roasting pretty much everything in the chili.

Using an earthy hop for this recipe really compliments the great pepper flavour, and works well in combination with the richness of the beans. If you'd prefer to make use of some fresh Fuggles - as one of the most popular home-grown hops - use about ½ cup, shredded in a food processor.

Makes about 22 cups

Poblano peppers	4	4
Anaheim pepper	1	1
Green bell peppers	3	3
Jalapeno peppers	4	4
Vegetable oil or spray		
Tomatillos	3 lbs	1500 g
Medium yellow onions	2	2
Garlic cloves, peeled	10	10
Vegetable oil	1 Tbsp	15 ml
Boneless pork tenderloin	3 lbs	1500 g
Chicken broth	4 cups	1 L
15oz cans blackeye peas, drained	2	2
15 oz cans small white beans, drained	4	4
Dried low-acid hop leaves	1/4 cup	50 ml
Salt and pepper		

Cilantro, hot sauce, and/or additional roasted jalapenos for garnish

Heat broiler to high

Slice all four kinds of pepper into large chunks, remove ribs and seeds. Arrange in a single layer on a broiling pan, brush or spray lightly with vegetable oil. Broil for a few minutes, until desired level of roasted. Repeat in batches until all peppers are roasted. Allow to cool.

Remove husks from tomatillos, wash well and remove any that don't look fresh/good. Slice each in half, arrange in a single layer on broiler pan, cut side up. Brush or spray with vegetable oil, broil until desired level of roast is achieved, repeating in batches till all are roasted. Cool.

Peel onions, slice into 1/2" slices. Arrange in a single layer on broiling pan – along with 6 of the 10 garlic cloves – brush or spray lightly with oil, broil until roasted enough, cool.

In a food processor, puree all of the roasted garlic along with about 1/3 of each type of peppers and onions, and about 1/2 the tomatillos. Set aside. Chop remaining vegetables into 1/2" chunks, set aside.

Trim your pork roast of excess fat, cut into ~ 1/2" chunks. In a large heavy pot, brown pork in vegetable oil. Once browned, add pureed vegetables, chopped vegetables, chicken broth, and beans. Finely mince or press remaining garlic cloves, add to the pot.

Heat chili almost to a boil, reduce heat and simmer gently for two hours, stirring every once in a while.

When simmering time is over, add hop leaves, stir well. Remove from heat, season with salt and pepper to taste. Garnish with your choice of toppings.

Condiments

Honey Hop Dipping Sauce

This is a fun dip, inspired by a Winnipeg favourite - honey dill sauce. This has a sweet start, a hoppy finish, and a delicate flavour - it's a great balance, and is amazing as a dip for chicken fingers, fries, corn dogs, and more.

Dry leaves - finely chopped (a coffee/spice grinder works well for this) - work the best for this recipe. If that's not an option, use 1/2-3/4 tsp powdered hop pellets, or 2 Tbsp finely chopped fresh hops. We like Cascade for this, but have fun playing with different varieties!

Makes 1 cup

Mayonnaise	2/3 cup	150 ml
Liquid Honey	1/3 cup	75 ml
Finely chopped dried hop leaves	1 Tbsp	15 ml
Salt	Pinch	Pinch

Mix together the mayonnaise and honey until smooth and well blended. Add hops and salt to the mayo mixture, stir well. Refrigerate for at least an hour to allow flavours to blend.

Chimichurri

Chimichurri is a popular Argentinian condiment - an herbal green sauce - most commonly used to dress up steak. Fresh parsley is combined with oil, vinegar, and other flavourings for a bright, "green"* flavour.

The addition of hops ups the complexity of the flavour profiles, while not taking anything away from the original, base recipe. We like using citrussy and/or herbal hops with this recipe - usually Sorachi Ace.

If you don't have access to dried hop leaves, you can substitute 1/4- ½ tsp ground hop pellets. When using pellets, I grind them and blitz them with just the oil and vinegar before adding the other ingredients, to ensure even dispersal.

* Yes, green can be a flavour, just like "blue" is a flavour :)

Makes about 1 cup of sauce

Italian (flat leaf) parsley, packed	2 cups	500 ml
Green onions	2	2
Dried hop leaves, crushed	2 tsp	10 ml
Olive oil	2/3 cup	150 ml
Red wine vinegar	1/4 cup	50 ml
Garlic cloves, pressed or finely minced	6	6
Salt	1 tsp	5 ml
Black pepper	1 tsp	5 ml
Crushed chilis / red pepper flakes	½ - 3/4 tsp	2-3 ml

Blitz all ingredients in a food processor until parsley leaves are finely chopped, but not PUREED.

Transfer to an air tight container, let sit at room temperature for at least two hours before using.

Chimichurri

Compound Butter

Compound butter is an extremely simple thing – you take a soft stick of butter, and mix stuff into it. Spices, fresh herbs, zest, finely chopped vegetables… whatever. Literally – WHATEVER… if you can think of some sort of flavourful aromatic, odds are you can make a compound butter with it.

The casual nature of that description doesn't really do justice to compound butter's place in cuisine – it's a very basic part of fine French cooking. Compound butters were made ahead of time to add flavour to almost any dish. Melted compound butter would serve as a substitute for a sauce, while room temperature butters would be served alongside steak, vegetables, seafood. Anchovy butter was (is?) quite popular, along with flavours such as truffle, tarragon, garlic… even wine.

Beyond historical use, compound butters are great in any modern kitchen. Given that compound butters can be made either sweet or savory, the possibilities are endless.

– Use compound butter on hot ears of fresh corn. Hop butter is a great way to give the corn a bit of zesty flavour, the hops compliment the corn flavour well, with the slight bitterness offsetting the sweetness of the corn.

– Spread on bread, alone or as part of a sandwich.

– Melt over popcorn! Seriously… probably our favorite use for it. You'll never want to use store bought powdered popcorn seasonings ever again!

This isn't so much a recipe, as it is a springboard for your own ideas and recipes. We like Kent Goulding as a nice "default" hop butter flavouring, but any hop would work well - have fun with it! In addition to varying to hop variety, you can add other peels, dried flowers, herbs, etc

Makes ½ lb

Butter, room temperature	½ lb	250 g
Dried hop leaves, ground	2-3 Tbsp	10-15 ml
Fresh lemon zest	½ -1 tsp	2-5 ml
Salt and pepper		

Whip butter until soft and smooth. Stir in hop leaves and zest, season with salt and pepper to taste.

Whip it until everything is well distributed. Refrigerate for about 10 minutes, or just long enough for it to firm up slightly – but still be workable. Turn it out onto a piece of plastic wrap or parchment paper, roll it into a log. (Alternatively, mush it into an appropriately sized ramekin or other vessel.) Chill until firmly set.

Try to use the butter within one week, if stored in the fridge. If you'd like to hang on to it for longer than that, it can be stored in the freezer for about a month.

Compound Butter

Honey Garlic-Hop Cooking Sauce

Growing up, I loved Honey Garlic sauce. It was really popular back home, used on everything from wings to meatballs to ribs. A sticky, sweet sauce... very much a comfort food.

As an adult expat, I reverse engineered the sauce, and was very happy with it - it was bang on!

The thing is, though... the sweetness of the source material - and my replication - can be obnoxious, and cloying to some. Because I love hops with garlic, I decided to try and cut the sweetness with a little bit of bitter kick. Oh, man... SO good.

This new and improved sauce is sweet, rich and flavourful. It adds a nice caramelized crust when meatballs are cooked in it, and is sure to become a new favourite for you, too!

We like Crystal hops for this, but you can use your favourite.. Or even a blend. Because of the thick sweetness of this, you can definitely get away with using a higher acid hop, if desired.

To use dried hops, blitz about 1-2 Tbsp through a spice grinder, and season to taste. 1/4 cup of fresh hops could be used instead of dried, shred them well in a food processor before adding.

Granulated sugar	1 cup	250 ml
Water	2/3 cup	150 ml
Honey	½ cup	125 ml
Molasses	1/4 cup	50 ml
Salt	1 tsp	5 ml
Lemon juice	1 tsp	5 ml
Garlic cloves, pressed or finely minced	6	6
Corn starch	2 tsp	10 ml
Pepper	Pinch	Pinch
Finely ground hop pellets	3/4 tsp	3 ml

Combine sugar, 1/3 cup of water, honey, molasses, salt, lemon juice, and garlic in a saucepan. Heat to a boil, stirring well to dissolve and combine ingredients. Once mixture boils, turn heat down and simmer for 5 minutes.

Whisk corn starch into remaining 1/3 cup of water, add to saucepan. Stir until well incorporated and mixture starts to thicken. Remove from heat, add hop powder, stir well.

At this point, you can use the sauce right away, or put it in the fridge for use within a couple of days. Strain out the garlic and hops, or don't – it's up to you!

Honey Garlic-Hop Cooking Sauce

Hop Honey

Hop honey is a unique condiment that is quick and easy to make. It works well on biscuits, cornbread, toast, and more.

It's even kind of pretty, sort of resembling the honeys you can buy that have pollen in them. You will likely have some of the hop powder rising to the top. You can stir this in before each use for extra flavour, or skim it off and discard, for a prettier presentation.

ANY kind of hop will work well in this, it just depends on what you're in the mood for. We tend to use Huell Melon, because we wanted the fruity tones to come through for the honey. It's a very mild hop in the honey though, and many others will punch through more if you're looking for something more hop forward. Citrus, floral, grassy, stone fruit, and tropical fruit aroma hops all work really well with this recipe.

Honey flavour will vary wildly based on what kind of flowers the bees were consuming, so try to pick hop flavours that will compliment what you're working with. For example, something like wildflower honey has a ton of pungent flavour, so you'll want a hop that won't get lost in that.

While I like to be able to give recommendations for using other forms of hops, for this recipe ... powdered pellets really do work best.

Makes 1 cup

Good quality liquid honey	1 cup	250 ml
Powdered hop pellets	1 tsp	5 ml
Salt	Pinch	Pinch

In a small saucepan, heat honey over medium heat until it's fairly runny.

Turn heat down to low, add hops, and stir well. Continue to cook for another 5 minutes.

Remove from heat and pour into a sterilized mini jam jar. Cover, cool to room temperature, then chill.

Hop Honey

Hopped IPA Hot Sauce

This isn't one of those "burn your mouth off for the sake of burning your mouth off" macho sauces. Don't get me wrong, it IS extremely hot.. but with a huge amount of actual flavour packed into it.

The roasting brings out a little sweetness and mellows out the peppers. The use of poblano and Anaheim peppers provides a bit more of a neutral base, so we could include the ghost and habanero peppers without being ridiculous about it.

The hops and IPA play off the sweetness and heat of the peppers, creating a really diverse flavour profile. It's a great all around hot sauce that can be used on almost anything!

If you'd like to experiment with making your own mix, you can throw our choice of peppers out the window, and combine your own. You'll want to use about 1 - 1 ½ lb worth, total. We tend to use Saaz hops, but really... your imagination is your only limit on this one.

Makes about 3.5 cups

Serrano peppers	5	5
Jalapeno peppers	3	3
Red jalapeno peppers	3	3
Poblano pepper	1	1
Anaheim pepper	1	1
Ghost pepper	1	1
Habanero pepper	1	1
Vegetable oil or spray		
Small onion	1	1
Garlic cloves, pressed or finely minced	6	6
White vinegar	1 cup	250 ml
IPA beer of choice	1 ½ cups	375 ml
Salt	1 Tbsp	15 ml
Powdered hop pellets	1 Tbsp	15 ml

Heat broiler to high. Slice all peppers into large chunks, remove ribs and seeds, slice onion into ½" thick slices.

Arrange vegetables in a single layer on a broiling pan, brush or spray lightly with vegetable oil. Broil for a few minutes, until desired level of roasted. Repeat in batches until all peppers and onion are roasted. Allow to cool.

Puree peppers, onion, garlic, and vinegar until very smooth. Add to a pot along with beer and salt. Bring mixture to a boil, simmer 25 minutes.

Add hops, puree mixture again for an even smoother texture. Taste, adjust salt if needed. Cool to room temperature before transferring to a bottle, chill.

Hopped IPA Hot Sauce

Hoppy IPA BBQ Sauce Recipe

Much like the Citrus IPA Glazed wings from earlier in this book, this BBQ sauce was developed on a past hop harvesting day, as a reward for all the hard word the guys were doing.

This was a recipe I'd conceptualized leading up to that day, and very much looked forward to seeing how it turned out. It's based with IPA and loaded with flavour from both fresh hops and citrus (juice and zest!), with a wonderfully complex taste ... while still being a legit BBQ sauce.

With the citrussy notes in this sauce, it worked ridiculously well on some grilled shrimp and scallops we made that night. It would also be great on pork and chicken, in particular – though I'm sure you could enjoy it on just about anything!

I'll let the guys give you their two (four?) cents on the sauce...

"This is a delicious sauce that has a great complexity. It starts out sweet with hints of orange and pepper then fades away with a delicious hop flavour. I don't think you need to be a hop-head to enjoy this, but if you are – like I am! – then this will be right up your alley. The flavours compliment each other so well and will taste great on almost anything. I'm pretty sure I could just grab a spoon and dig into the jar when nobody is looking." – Porter

"Being a Midwesterner, I had never had any seafood with BBQ sauce on it. Sure, I've had ribs or pork slathered in the stuff but never any fish ... let alone shellfish.

I have to say the smell and look of the shrimp was amazing, nicely seared with a light brushing of sauce. I was excited for the first bite. It was fantastic, the tangy smokey flavour was certainly making a showing, followed by the hot spicy flavours I love in any BBQ sauce, then the hops took the end and merged all the flavours with that of the shrimp. Just like a good hoppy pint of joy, the front, middle and end were present.

Maybe it was because of the addition of the hops that I noticed this more than I have in other foods as a hop head I always look for more of a flavour profile in my beer than I usually do my food, but its addition definitely added excitement, taste and enjoyment. I was so surprised and would definitely keep an eye out for more foods and recipes with hops to try." – Trevor

Because I created this recipe specifically for the harvest, I made use of the fresh (wet) Centennial hops we had available. You could also use dried hop leaves - about 1/4 cup - or hop pellets - about 1-2 tsp, powdered.

Makes about 3 cups

Olive oil	1 Tbsp	15 ml
Small red onion, grated or finely chopped	½	½
Jalapeno pepper, grated or finely chopped	1	1
IPA beer of choice	1 cup	250 ml
Fresh hops, divided	½ cup	125 ml
Garlic cloves, pressed or finely minced	2	2
Ketchup	2 cups	500 ml
Apple cider vinegar	½ cup	125 ml
Orange juice	2 Tbsp	30 ml
Orange, zest of	½ - 1	½ - 1
Brown sugar, packed	½ cup	125 ml
Granulated sugar	2 Tbsp	30 ml
Black pepper	1 tsp	5 ml
Mustard powder	½ tsp	2 ml

Saute onion and jalapeno in olive oil until translucent. Add beer, 1/4 cup of hops, and garlic, simmer for 5 minutes. Add all remaining ingredients except for the 1/4 cup of reserved hops. Stir well, turn heat down to low, cover and simmer for 1 hour – stirring frequently.

Add remaining hops, simmer for 5 more minutes. Press sauce through wire strainer, discarding solids left behind. Chill until use.

Hoppy IPA BBQ Sauce Recipe

Mango Habanero Sauce

Given how well hops worked with my Citrus IPA wings, I decided a while back that they'd also make a great addition to one of my favourite wing sauces - Mango Habanero sauce.

I wasn't wrong!

Sweet and spicy is even better when you add a little bitter to the mix, balancing everything out. The combination is fabulous in this recipe. Hops and spicy food go so well together in general, after all - it's why IPAs are recommended for eating with wings. We like to use Cascade pellets for this, but really - any citrus or peppery hop variety will taste

I like to use canned mango pulp in this sauce, as it's great year-round, and far less work than dealing with fresh mangos. I use Swad Kesar brand, which is actually sweetened - so a straight puree won't work as a substitute, sorry about that! This brand is readily available in Indian grocery stores, as well as the ethnic foods aisle of many large grocers.

This sauce tastes REALLY hot right off a spoon, but once you pour it over wings, it's got a nice kick - but it's a refined kick. It's not hot for the sake of being hot, it's got great flavour

Makes about 4.5 cups

Small onion	1	1
Garlic cloves, pressed or finely minced	3	3
Habanero peppers	2-3	2-3
Olive oil	2 Tbsp	30 ml
Tomato paste	½ cup	125 ml
Can sweetened mango pulp	30 oz	850 g
Liquid honey	½ cup	125 ml
Cider vinegar	1/3 cup	75 ml
Limes, juice of	2	2
Powdered hop pellets	1 tsp	5 ml
Salt and pepper		

Finely chop onion, garlic, and habanero peppers. Add to a medium saucepan along with olive oil, cook over medium heat until soft. Add tomato paste and continue to cook, stirring constantly, until mixture begins to brown a little.

Stir in everything else except hops, salt, and pepper. Bring just to a boil, reduce heat and simmer, stirring often, for 20 minutes, or until mixture has thickened. Add hops, stir well, remove from heat and allow to sit for 10 minutes.

Puree in a blender, food processor, or with immersion blender until smooth. Season with salt and pepper to taste. Transfer to clean jar, store in fridge for up to 3 weeks.

Mango Habanero Sauce

Hopped Pepper Jelly

In general, pepper jelly is one of our favourite jellies, we love it on crackers with cream cheese. I mean, we'll go through absolutely ridiculous amounts of it, shortly after any batch I put on. When hops are added to the mix, though, the whole thing is elevated - the hops cut the sweetness of it, adding balance. We like earthy and or citrussy hops with this, and tend to use Fuggle. If you use a very low alpha acid hop, you can use a fair amount of it, as we call for - it's pretty in the jar.

Makes 6 jam jars

Poblano pepper	1	1
Green bell pepper	1	1
Jalapeno peppers	2	2
Anaheim peppers	2	2
Vinegar	1 ½ cups	375 ml
Granulated sugar	6 cups	1500 ml
Liquid pectin	1 pouch	1 pouch
Dried hop leaves, low acid	1 cup	250 ml

Remove stems, cores, and seeds from all peppers, chop into large chunks. Put all peppers in food processor, process till finely chopped. Put peppers and vinegar into pot, bring to boil. After 1 minute, turn temperature down and simmer another 15 minutes.

Strain peppers for the juice - I like to line a metal colander with a coffee filter for this. Discard the solids, return pepper juice to the pot. Add sugar to strained pepper juice. Turn heat up to medium-high, and stir constantly while bringing it to a rapid boil.

Remove from heat, add pectin and hops. Stir well. Fill a large pot with at least 6" of water, put on medium or high heat to bring it to a boil as you prepare your jars.

Pour jelly into sterilized jam jars, leaving about 1/8" inch space on top. Wipe off the top edges of the jar with a clean, wet towel, top each with a new, sterilized lid, and carefully screw on a clean lid ring. I like to use a kitchen towel for this, the jars are HOT!

Carefully place your jars of jelly into the boiling water pot, allow to process for 5 minutes. CAREFULLY remove them, allow to cool overnight.

The next morning, check to make sure that all of the jars achieved a proper seal – try to push down in the middle of each lid. If it "pops", it did not seal. Any jars that didn't seal should be put in the fridge and used in the next few weeks. This won't be difficult to do!

Tighten all lids. Jelly should keep for around a year.

Hopped Pepper Jelly

Hoppy Dill Pickle Relish

A few years ago, on one of my pickling binges - and fresh off getting my husband addicted to my hoppy IPA pickles - I decided that I should make a hopped up version of pickle relish. We love (non-sweet!) dill pickle relish, this would be a fun variant on the old favorite.

I wanted to have a bit of fun with it, and make it visually different from my normal dill pickle recipe. The addition of turmeric turned it a lovely golden colour, while the flecks of red from the sweet red peppers worked well to help create a … pretty? … relish. Yes, that works – In the jar, this is a really pretty relish.

The flavour on this is wonderful, and would pair well with a variety of meats – well beyond the traditional use on a hotdog. I may actually prefer this to dill relish! The bitterness from the hops just really works well in this context.

We used dried Centennial hops for this, but you can use almost any variety. For fresh hops, use about ½ cup worth.

Makes about 3 pints

Pickling cucumbers, cleaned	2 lbs	1 kg
Small onion, peeled	1	1
Small red pepper	1	1
Jalapeno peppers	1-2	1-2
Vinegar	2 cups	500 ml
Dried hop leaves	1/4 cup	50 ml
Pickling / canning salt	1/4 cup	50 ml
Garlic cloves, pressed or finely minced	3	3
Mustard seed	1 tsp	5 ml
Celery seed	½ tsp	2 ml
Dill seed	1/4 tsp	1 ml
Turmeric	1/4 tsp	1 ml

Chop cucumbers, onion, red pepper and jalapeno peppers into approximately 1" pieces, blitz in a food processor until finely chopped.

Fill a large pot with at least 6" of water, put on medium or high heat to bring it to a boil as you prepare your relish..

In another heavy pot, bring vinegar to a boil. Add hops and stir well, mashing them around a bit. Allow them to simmer for 5-10 minutes, tasting frequently.

Once mixture has reached your desired level of bitterness, use a slotted spoon to remove all hop leaves. Add processed vegetables and all remaining ingredients, bring mixture to a boil.

Use a sterile ladle and canning funnel, pour boiling relish into sterilized jars, leaving about ½" of head space.

Wipe off the top edges of the jars with a clean, wet towel, top each with a new, sterilized lid, and carefully screw on a clean lid ring. I like to use a kitchen towel for this, the jars are HOT! Carefully place your jars of relish into the boiling water pot, allow to process for 15 minutes. CAREFULLY remove them, allow to cool overnight.

The next morning, check to make sure that all of the jars achieved a proper seal – try to push down in the middle of each lid. If it "pops", it did not seal. Any jars that didn't seal should be put in the fridge and used in the next few weeks.

Store in a cool, dark area for up to 1 year, chill well before eating.

Hoppy Dill Pickle Relish

Salsa Verde

We like our salsa verde roasted, and tend to char the ingredients over charcoal. If this isn't an option, feel free to grill over propane, or roast them under your broiler. If you have wood chips to smoke/grill with, use them – we tend to use applewood chips. We like Kent Goulding hops for these, but many varieties would work well. If you'd like to use powdered pellet hops, use about ½ tsp, or to taste. If using fresh, blitz about 1/3 cup worth through a food processor, before adding to the pot.

Makes about 3 cups

Tomatillos	1 ½ lb	750 g
Medium white onion	1	1
Poblano peppers	2	2
Green bell pepper	1	1
Jalapeno peppers	1-2	1-2
Olive oil		
Garlic cloves, peeled	4	4
Lime, zest and juice of	½	½
Granulated sugar	1 tsp	5 ml
Dry hop leaves (Kent Goulding)	1 Tbsp	15 ml
Salt and pepper		

Heat your grill – I like to use charcoal for this, but propane is fine also. Turn your (oven) broiler up to high. While everything is heating, prepare your vegetables to roast:

Prepare a couple cookie sheets with foil or parchment paper. Remove husks from tomatillos, wash well and remove any that don't look fresh/good. Slice each in half, arrange in a single layer on baking sheets, toss garlic cloves in amongst the tomatillos. Roast tomatillos under the broiler until as charred as you would like. Pour off excess juices, allow to cool.

Slice onions into 1/2" thick slices, slice poblano and bell peppers into large flat pieces. Cut jalapenos in half, scooping out seeds and ribs if you want a more mild salsa.

Brush peppers with olive oil, then grill everything until as "done" as you would like – personally, I like some dark grill marks for this, but not an overall char.. Remove items as they are ready – the peppers will cook the fastest. Allow everything to cool.

Drain tomatillos and garlic of any newly accumulated juices, run through a food processor until rough chopped, place in a large pot.

Chop peppers and onion - I use a food processor for this. Add peppers and onion to the pot, along with lime juice & zest, and sugar, stir well. Bring to a boil, cook for about 10 minutes, or until mixture thickens.

Remove from heat, stir in hop leaves. Season with salt and pepper to taste, chill before eating.

Salsa Verde

Steak Sauce

Wonderfully rich and complex. The onion and citrus come through well, complimenting the hops. The smoked serrano brings a bit of a kick, and a hint of smokiness.

We tend to use Sterling hops with this, but any relatively low acid variety of hops with earthy, herbal, or citrus aroma would work well.

Makes about 2 1/2 cups

Celery stalk	1	1
Small onion	½	½
Seedless orange, pulp of	½	½
Olive oil	1 Tbsp	15 ml
Garlic cloves, pressed or finely minced	3-4	3-4
Cider vinegar	½ cup	125 ml
Dijon mustard	1/3 cup	75 ml
Dark brown sugar, packed	1/4 cup	50 ml
Canned tomato puree	2 cups	500 ml
Raisins	½ cup	125 ml
Smoked serrano powder	½ + tsp	2 + ml
Powdered hop pellets	2 tsp	10 ml
Liquid smoke	5 drops	5 drops
Salt and pepper		

Puree onion, celery, orange pulp, and garlic, add to a pot along with olive oil. Cook over medium-high heat, stirring until vegetables are soft and starting to caramelize.

Add everything else except hops, liquid smoke, salt, and pepper. Stir well to combine.

Bring mixture to a boil, turn heat down to medium low. Simmer for 20 minutes, stirring frequently. Remove from heat, add hops, and allow to cool for 10 minutes.

Puree sauce in a blender or food processor until smooth-ish.

Add liquid smoke, season with salt and pepper to taste. Add more smoked serrano powder and/or liquid smoke if desired.

Cool to room temperature before transferring to a clean jar - keep refrigerated.

Steak Sauce

Salad Dressings

Given how well hops accent vegetables, obviously we had to create a dressing recipe or two! We chose two styles of dressing that were heavily based on "green" flavours - Ranch and Italian. Many / most hop varieties would work well with these recipes, just aim for a low acid variety If you'd like to use dried hop leaves, finely chop/grind them before measuring about 1 tsp into the recipe. For fresh hops, you can use about 2 tsp of finely chopped leaves.

Ranch Dressing

Makes about 2 cups

Mayonnaise	3/4 cup	175 ml
Sour cream	3/4 cup	175 ml
Buttermilk	1/3 cup	75 ml
Fresh dill, chopped	1/4 cup	50 ml
Fresh parsley, chopped	2 Tbsp	30 ml
Fresh chives, chopped	2 Tbsp	30 ml
Dijon mustard	1 Tbsp	15 ml
Cider vinegar	1 tsp	5 ml
Paprika	1/4 tsp	1 ml
Powdered hop pellets	1/4 tsp	1 ml
Garlic cloves, pressed or finely minced	2	2
Green onion, finely chopped	1	1
Salt and pepper		

Measure all ingredients - except salt and pepper - into a blender, blitz to combine. Season with salt and pepper to taste, add more hop powder if you like.

Italian Dressing

Makes about 1 1/3 cups

Olive oil	1 cup	250 ml
Red wine vinegar	1/4 cup	50 ml
Dried oregano	1 ½ tsp	7 ml
Onion powder	1 tsp	5 ml
Dried basil	½ tsp	2 ml
Red pepper flakes	½ tsp	2 ml
Powdered hop pellets	1/4 tsp	1 ml
Garlic cloves, pressed or finely minced	4	4
Lemon, zest and juice of	1	1
Dried thyme	Pinch	Pinch
Salt and pepper		

Measure all ingredients - except salt and pepper - into a blender, blitz to combine. Season with salt and pepper to taste, add more hop powder if you like. Chill, shake well before using.

Salad Dressings

Hop Salts

Infused salts are gaining popularity in kitchens all across North America, and for good reason - they bring a little extra something to a dish, especially when sprinkled as a finishing salt.

There are many ways to make hop infused salts. Some are fairly instant, some require a lot of patience. Some just look like coloured salt, while others can have bits of hop visible - it's all about what you're going for!

This is less a recipe, and more a set of... guidelines. Suggestions, really!

Slow Infusions

For hop salt that just looks like tinted salt, you'll want to do a slow infusion. Spread salt of choice- in a container that will seal airtight. Gently spread a layer of fresh or dried hop cones on top, and layer with more salt. Cover, and store in a cool , dark place for at least 1 month.

Taste for doneness - if it's hoppy enough, gently sift out the hops, and transfer salt to an airtight spice jar. If you'd like it more hoppy, re-seal the lid, and allow to infuse as long as you'd like.

Quick Infusions

For fairly instant "infusions", you'll basically just be mixing the hops with the salt, and allowing to infuse for a day or two before use. To make, blitz together 1 cup of salt - sea or table, fine, flake, or coarse - with either 1/4 cup of dried hop leaves, or 2 tsp powdered hop pellets. Taste, adjust amount of hops if desired.

Smoked Hop Salts

For added flavour, hop salts can be smoked after infusing - and is particularly great as a popcorn topping.

To smoke salt, get foil sheet pan, or make one by rolling the edges up on a piece of foil. Place on the rack of a smoker, spread salt out in a thin layer. Cold smoke - stirring every hour or so - until desired flavour is reached, between 4 and 12 hours.

Storage

Hop salts - slow or quick infusions, smoked or not - can be stored in an airtight container for up to 4 months for best results. Salt will begin to lose its flavour, but will still be edible for long past the 4th month.

Hop Salts

Salted Hop Caramels

Desserts

Salted Hop Caramels

The sweet/salt/bitter combination of these candies is a great one - soft caramels with a subtle but distinct difference to them. Like many of the recipes in this book, most people wouldn't be able to pick it out as specifically being hop flavoured, it's just a mellow, refined taste that's unlike anything you'd get from the more traditional extracts.

Having a well calibrated candy thermometer goes a long way to ensuring success when making caramels - If the mixture isn't hot enough, it won't set enough to cut, and if it boils too hot, it will form hard caramels, rather than soft.

Makes about 2.5 lbs of candy

Shortening or butter, for preparation		
Baking spray		
Granulated sugar	2 cups	500 ml
Heavy whipping cream	2 cups	500 ml
Light brown sugar, packed	1 cup	250 ml
Corn syrup	1 cup	250 ml
Evaporated milk	1 cup	250 ml
Butter	1 cup	250 ml
Hop extract	1 Tbsp	15 ml
Salt	½ tsp	2 ml

Candy wrappers or waxed paper squares

Grease a large cookie pan (with walls), set aside. Lightly spray the inside of a large pot.

In sprayed pot, combine all ingredients except hop extract and salt. Cook over medium heat, stirring constantly, until butter melts and mixture is smooth. Affix a candy thermometer to the inside of the pot, so that it is IN the mixture, but not touching the bottom of the pot.

Cook, gently stirring frequently, until mixture reaches 250F (120 C). Remove from heat, stir in hop extract and salt until well combined.

Pour mixture into greased cookie pen, allow to cool completely.

Use a clean knife or kitchen scissors to cut until bite sized pieces, wrap in purchased candy wrappers or waxed paper.

Hopped Jalapeno Beer Brittle

"Do you have one of those icons for a little halo over it? You should use it for this" - hubby.

My jalapeno beer brittle has been a popular favourite - in this house, among friends, and on my blog - for many years now. We love the "savoury" addition of jalapenos and beer to such a traditional candy recipe. This is a recipe that even people who hate beer end up loving!

The addition of hops to the recipe not only amplifies the presence of the beer, but it cuts through some of the sugar for a layered, balanced effect. Tree distinct flavours come through - the caramelized jalapenos come through first - not a hot thing, just a bit of earthy warmness. Then you can taste beer, and then it ends in a crescendo of hop flavour. It's really fun, how the flavours come in waves!

We tend to use Kent Goulding or Centennial hops for this candy.

Makes about 1.5 lb of candy

Cooking Spray		
Granulated sugar	1 cup	250 ml
Light corn syrup	½ cup	125 ml
IPA beer	1/3 cup	75 ml
Salt	1/4 tsp	1 ml
Jalapeno peppers, seeded and finely chopped	1-2	1-2
Baking soda	1 tsp	5 ml
Butter	2 Tbsp	30 ml
Roasted, salted peanuts	1 ½ cup	375 ml
Dry hop leaves - we used Kent Goulding.	1/4-1/3 cup	50-75 ml

Set oven to "warm", or lowest temperature. Spray a large cookie sheet with cooking spray. Place inside warm oven.

In a heavy saucepan (2 quart), mix together sugar, corn syrup, beer, salt, and jalapeno pepper bits. Bring to boil over medium-high heat, then attach candy thermometer to saucepan. Stir often until temperature reaches 300 F (150 C). Keep a close eye on it after about 280 (140 C) degrees, as the temp has a tendency to race up at that point. If you turn your back, you could burn it!

At 300 F (150 C), remove the pan from heat, add baking soda and butter, stir until well incorporated. Quickly add in peanuts and hop leaves and stir until completely coated.

Remove cookie sheet from oven, and pour brittle out onto it. Working very quickly, use 2 buttered forks to pull the brittle mixture out from the center, till it is thinly spread and relatively even.

Cool completely, then break into pieces.

Hopped Jalapeno Beer Brittle

Hopped Brownies

The slightly bitter finish works really well with the rich chocolate taste, especially with the addition of the brown sugar. It brightens it up, so the heaviness of the brownie isn't cloying.

We used "Special Dark" cocoa, and extract made from Citra® hops for this. You can use regular cocoa powder if you'd like - it'll just make a slightly lighter coloured brownie.

Makes one 9x13 pan of brownies

Cocoa powder	1 cup	250 ml
Granulated sugar	1 cup	250 ml
Light brown sugar, packed	1 cup	250 ml
All purpose flour*	1 cup	250 ml
Salt	½ tsp	2 ml
Large eggs	4	4
Butter, melted	1 cup	250 ml
Hop extract	2 tsp	10 ml
Milk Chocolate chips	2 cup	500 ml

Frosting:

Powdered (confectioners / icing) sugar	2 cups	500 ml
Cocoa powder	2 Tbsp	20 ml
Salt	Pinch	Pinch
Milk	3 Tbsp	45 ml
Hop extract	2-3 tsp	10-15 ml

Preheat oven to 350F (180 C). Prepare 9 x 13 pan (or two 8 x 8" pans) with pan spray or shortening.

In large mixing bowl, combine first five ingredients. Add beaten eggs , melted butter, and hop extract, stir until dry ingredients are well incorporated and wet. Add chocolate chips, stir until evenly distributed in the batter.

Spread batter into prepared pan(s), Bake for 20 – 25 minutes for 8 x 8" pans, or 30-35 minutes for 9 x 13" pan. Brownies are done when knife inserted into center comes out clean. Let cool completely

Whisk together powdered sugar, cocoa powder, and salt. Add milk and hop extract, whisk to form a thick, smooth frosting. Heat in microwave for 15 seconds, pour/spread on cooled brownies. Allow to set before cutting and serving.

*For gluten free: Swap out the all purpose flour for

Light buckwheat flour	½ cup	125 ml
Sorghum flour	1/4 cup	50 ml
Coconut flour	1/4 cup	50 ml

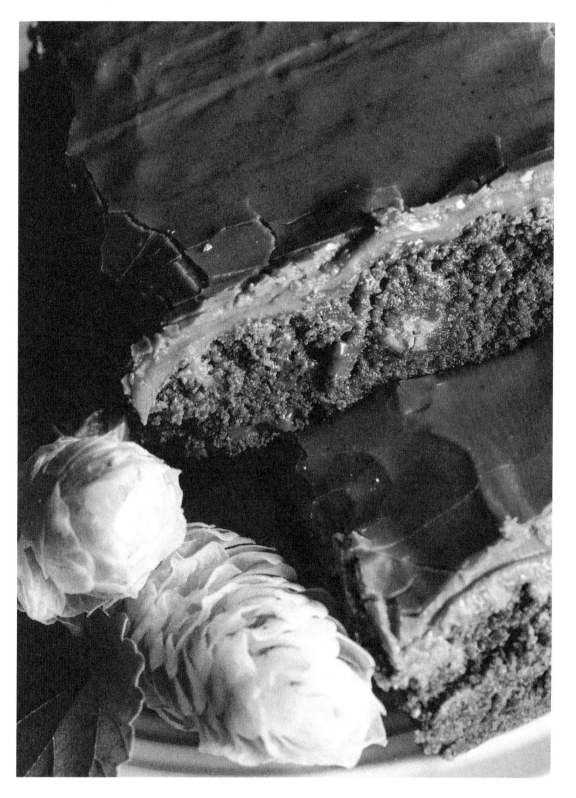

Hopped Brownies

Hop Sorbet

Sorbet is popular as a "diet friendly" dessert, as it doesn't have any of the fat found in ice cream. Depending on the area, this is also sometimes referred to as sherbet (which isn't actually the same thing!) Italian ice, etc.

Instantly put a smile on porter's face. Freshly made sorbet is always amazing on its own, but the little tingle of that something EXTRA from the hops really kicks it up to something special. We have made this both with Northern Brewer pellet hops, and with our Citra® extract, and both were amazing. If using extract, skip the steeping, and add the extract after straining out the zest solids - 1tsp, or to taste.

Makes about 2 quarts.

Granulated sugar	1 ½ cups	375 ml
Water	1 cup	250 ml
Orange, zest of	1	1
Lemon, zest and juice of	1	1
Lime, zest and juice of	1	1
Orange juice	3 cups	750 ml
Hop pellets	1 Tbsp	15 ml

In a large saucepan, combine sugar, water, and citrus zest. Heat to a simmer, stirring until all of the sugar is dissolved. Turn heat down to low, allow to simmer very gently for 10 minutes.

Remove syrup from heat. Add juices and hops, allow to steep for 3 minutes. Strain through fine cheesecloth and/or a coffee filter, discard solids.

Allow sorbet to cool to room temperature, then transfer to fridge to chill thoroughly. Follow your ice cream maker's instructions to freeze fruit mixture.

Serve immediately for a soft sorbet, or freeze for at least 1 hour for a more firm sorbet.

If recipe produces more than your ice cream maker can handle in one batch, keep any extra fruit mixture chilled until use - process into frozen sorbet within a day or two.

Hop Sorbet

Hop Infused Dark Chocolate Truffles

These truffles were one of two recipes that got this whole thing started, back in 2010. My husband had recently harvested his first year hops, and there wasn't really enough to brew anything with... so we discussed making something else. I'd been on a truffle making kick at the time, so it seemed obvious what we should make.

They were great! The first time around, we used Centennial, but have moved to preferring Columbus hops for this. Many/most, if not all hop varieties would work well as a truffle flavouring.

If you'd prefer, you can use whole fresh hops, as we did that first time: about 6-8 cones worth, or a handful of dried hops. (Highly precise, I know - taste as you go!)

Good quality semi-sweet chocolate chips	12 oz	375 g
Heavy whipping cream	3/4 cup	175 ml
Finely ground hop pellets	1/4 tsp	1 ml
Butter	3 Tbsp	45 ml
Granulated sugar	2 Tbsp	30 ml
Cocoa (We used Hershey's Special Dark)		

Place chocolate chips into a glass mixing bowl, and set aside.

On stove top, bring heavy whipping cream, hop pellets, and butter to a light simmer. Remove from heat, allow to steep for about 10 minutes. Be sure to taste as you go – you may not want to use the whole 10 minute steeping time.

Once steeping time is complete, bring to just a simmer again.

Strain hot cream mixture through 2 layers of cheesecloth, and into bowl of chocolate chips, discarding hop pulp. Let mixture sit for 3-5 minutes. Starting in the middle of the bowl, slowly start stirring the chocolate and cream until all of the chocolate is melted, with the cream completely incorporated into it – it should be smooth.

Cover with plastic wrap, preferably resting right on top of the surface – this prevents a skin from forming while it cools. Chill in the fridge for at least two hours, until it's pretty solid.

Once solid, scoop out small amounts (a teaspoon or so), and roll them into balls. Try to handle the chocolate as quickly as possible, or it will melt.

Wash and dry hands, then roll ganache centers in cocoa. Store in an airtight container for up to 1 week.

Hop Infused Dark Chocolate Truffles

Hopped Lemon Meringue Pie

Lemon and hops are always amazing together. The richness of the custard really balances well with the inclusion of hops, which complements and contrasts with it at the same time. The citrus of the hops pairs well, while the bright herbal tones richness of the custard. Definitely not like anything you get from a boxed pie filling mix!

The key to any successful lemon meringue pie is timing. To prevent weeping - liquid coming out from undercooked meringue, separating the meringue from the lemon filling and generally making a mess - the meringue must be spread over HOT pie filling, and immediately baked.

Makes 1 9" pie

Granulated sugar	1 ½ cup	375 ml
Cornstarch	1/3 cup	75 ml
Salt	1/4 tsp	1 ml
Milk	2 cups	500 ml
Lemons, zest and juice of	3	3
Large egg yolks, beaten	7	7
Butter	3 Tbsp	45 ml
Hop extract	1 Tbsp	15 ml
Large egg whites	7	7
Granulated sugar	2/3 cup	150 ml
Salt	Pinch	Pinch

1 (9 inch) pie crust, baked and cooled

Preheat oven to 350 F (180 C).

Whisk together sugar, cornstarch, and salt until well combined, with no lumps. Add to a medium saucepan, along with milk, lemon juice (should be about 1 cup), lemon zest, and egg yolks. Whisk well, set aside for a moment.

In a stand mixer - or a large bowl with a hand mixer - combine egg whites, sugar, and salt. Beat egg white mixture until stiff peaks form.

As egg whites are beating, bring lemon mixture to a boil over medium high heat, stirring constantly. Once mixture boils, reduce heat to low and continue to stir until mixture reaches desired thickness. Remove from heat, add butter and hop extract, and stir well to melt butter and combine.

Spoon hot lemon mixture into cooled, pre-baked pie shell. Immediately spread meringue over pie filling, completely covering all exposed filling. Bake for 15 minutes, or until edges of meringue are golden. Cool to room temperature before refrigerating - UNCOVERED - for two hours before serving.

Hopped Lemon Meringue Pie

Hopped Cheesecake with Citrus Glaze

It's probably no surprise, at this point, that I like Citra ® hops for this - it's a strong, bright citrus flavour with a bitterness that cuts through what can be a cloyingly rich, sweet dessert. At the levels called for, this makes a very balanced, elegant dessert.

You'd never pick the flavour out as being hops - it's definitely citrussy, but doesn't taste like orange, or lemon. Very sophisticated, almost like ... using some exotic fruit that no one has ever heard of. This is by far my favourite cheesecake ever - and that's saying something!

Makes 1 9" cheesecake

Graham crumbs (can use gluten-free!)	1 ½ cup	375 ml
Granulated sugar	1/4 cup	50 ml
Butter, melted	5 Tbsp	75 ml
Cream cheese, room temperature	2 lbs	1000 g
Granulated sugar	1 ½ cup	375 ml
Sour cream	1 cup	250 ml
Heavy cream	1 cup	250 ml
Large eggs	6	6
Lemon, juice of	1	1
Hop extract	1 Tbsp	15 ml
Citrus marmalade of choice	1 cup	250 ml
Lemon, juice and zest of	1	1
Hop extract	1 tsp	5 ml
Salt	Pinch	Pinch

Combine graham cracker crumbs, sugar, and butter until completely mixed & moistened. Evenly distribute across the bottom of a 9"spring form pan. Press firmly, extending crust partway up the sides of the pan. Chill for at least 1 hour.

Preheat oven to 425 F (220 C)

In stand mixer, beat together cream cheese and sugar just until smooth. Add sour cream, heavy cream, eggs, lemon juice, and extract. Beat on low / medium-low just until smooth. Gently pour batter into prepared crust. Chill for 10 minutes.

Bake cheesecake for 15 minutes. After 15 minutes, turn the oven down to 325 F (160 C) and bake for 50 minutes. Once baking time is complete, turn off the oven and allow cake to cool - WITHOUT opening the door! - for 2 hours. Chill cake thoroughly.

Whisk together marmalade, lemon juice, zest, hop extract, and salt in a small saucepan. Heat over medium just until sauce is well combined, smooth, and liquid. Pour over chilled cake, return to fridge for at least 10 minutes before slicing and serving.

Hopped Cheesecake with Citrus Glaze

Hop Flavoured Beer Lollipops

Back in 2010, I developed this recipe, on a lark. We'd just harvested our first "crop" (using the term very generously!) of Centennial hops, and I was playing with them. It was one of my very first experiments with using hops in candy making, even before I started cooking with them.

They were great! I dubbed them "Lollihops" (A name that was swiped by a very rude candy company 4 years later!), and blogged the recipe - it's been a popular one, both on the blog, and in "The Spirited Baker".

If you'd prefer, you can use dried hops instead - about 1/4 cup worth. I don't recommend using pellets for this recipe. Alternately, you can skip all the infusion and add 2 tsp of hop extract after removing pan from heat, just before dropping into lollipops.

Butter		
IPA beer of choice	½ cup	125 ml
Fresh hop cones	10	10
Granulated sugar	1 cup	250 ml
Light corn syrup	½ cup	125 ml
Lollipop sticks		

Use butter to generously grease the back of 1 or 2 baking sheets, set aside.

Heat beer to a light simmer. Break up hop cones into leaves, add to warm beer. Remove from heat, allow to simmer for about 10 minutes. (Be sure to taste as you go – you may not want to use the whole 10 minute steeping time.)

Strain beer into a measuring glass, measuring only 1/3 cup, discard solids and excess beer. (The ½ cup measurement is to allow for some evaporation / hop leaf absorption). In a heavy saucepan, mix together sugar, corn syrup, and strained 1/3 cup of beer.

Bring to boil over medium-high heat, then attach candy thermometer to saucepan. Stir often until temperature reaches 300 F (150 C). Keep a very close eye on it after about 280 F (120 C), as the temperature has a tendency to race up at that point. If you turn your back, you could burn it!

At 300 F (150 C), remove the pan from heat. Allow to cool & thicken slightly, stirring constantly – about 1 minute.

Working quickly, drop small amounts of the hot sugar mixture onto the greased baking sheets – about 1-3 tsp(s) per, depending on the desired size of your lollihops.

Lay a lollipop stick into each circle, so that the tip is near the center of the lollipop, and flat against the surface. (ie, you want it laying on the baking sheet, not sticking up from it!). Carefully give each stick a bit of a twirl, so that the candy coats around the stick to hold it in place. Allow to harden before removing from baking sheet. Wrap in plastic squares.

Hop Flavoured Beer Lollipops

Hopped Chocolate Mousse

Chocolate and citrus are well known to go together, so hop extract made from citrussy varieties really works well for this chocolate mousse. It has a far more complex flavour than just adding orange extract - Elegant!

Amarillo® hops are our favourite for this - we like the bit of floral aroma with the light, fluffy chocolate.

Makes 4-6 servings

Heavy cream	2 cups	500 ml
Butter	4 Tbsp	60 ml
Granulated sugar	4 Tbsp	60 ml
Finely ground hop pellets	1 tsp	5 ml
Semi sweet chocolate chips	12 oz	375 g
Unflavoured gelatin powder	1 tsp	5 ml
Cold water	1/3 cup	75 ml
Vanilla extract	1 tsp	5 ml

On stove top, bring heavy whipping cream, butter, and sugar to a light simmer. Remove from heat, add hops, and allow to steep for about 10 minutes. Be sure to taste as you go – you may not want to use the whole 10 minute steeping time.

Strain hot cream mixture through 2 layers of cheesecloth, discarding hop pulp. Return mixture to pot, heat back up to a simmer.

Add chocolate, stir well, and remove from heat. Allow to sit for 2 minutes, before continuing stirring until chocolate is completely melted and mixture is smooth.

Cool chocolate mixture to room temperature, then cover and chill until cold, at least 2 hours.

In a small, microwave safe bow, sprinkle gelatin over water, allow to sit for 5 minutes. Transfer bowl to microwave, heat in 10 second increments until gelatin dissolves into the water.

Whip chilled chocolate mixture until stiff peaks form, then carefully fold in the and gelatin mixture, gently stirring until combined.

Pour into serving glasses, chill until set, about 2 hours. Serve cold.

Hopped Chocolate Mousse

Hoppy Citrus French Macarons

Hoppy Citrus French Macarons

A sudden craving for macarons that hit right around the time our hop harvest was seriously taking over our yard one year resulted in the creation of this recipe!

I've always found that commercially available macarons don't tend to have enough flavour for my liking - well, the presence of hops sure fixed that problem!

This was before I started making and using hop extracts, which could definitely be used as a clean, easy substitute for ground hop leaves. You can use about 1 tsp of hop extract, or ½ tsp of finely ground pellets, if you like. We used Cascade hops, which are known for their citrussy notes - but many hop varieties would work well. If using dry hop leaves, grind to a fine powder in a spice or coffee grinder.

If SUPER hoppy IPAs are your thing, you could increase the amount of hops in this recipe by a little - taste and see what you think. My husband loves this with double the hops, but that's not really a universally acceptable level of bitterness!

Makes 20-24 cookies

Powdered (confectioners / icing) sugar	1 ½ cup	375 ml
Finely ground almonds	1 cup	250 ml
Finely ground dried hop leaves	1 Tbsp	15 ml
Large egg whites	3	3
Granulated sugar	4 Tbsp	60 ml
Green gel food colouring, if desired		

Preheat your oven to 300 F (150 C). Line 2 cookie sheets with parchment paper.

Mix together powdered sugar, ground almonds, and hop powder. Sift through a wire strainer, discarding any large pieces. Set aside.

Mix egg whites and sugar in a very clean metal mixer bowl. It is very important that not only are the bowl and whisk attachment VERY clean, but that no specks of egg yolk are included with the egg white. The presence of any egg yolk or grease on your bowl or whisk will prevent the egg whites from properly whipping up. This is the only macaron "rule" you really need to be concerned about!

Affix your bowl to the mixer, and whip eggs on high until stiff peaks form. The whites will be pillowy, thick, and marshmallowy. When you remove the whisk from the meringue, it should leave a very definite "peak" – if the tip flips over a little, that's ok. Add a small amount food colouring, if desired, whisk in.

Dump bowl of dry ingredients into the meringue. Use a wooden spoon or spatula to gently stir the mixture until everything is well incorporated and very thick.

Once mixture is fairly uniform, beat it until it's still thick, but oozes a bit. You don't want to beat it till it's fully RUNNY, but you'd like it to settle back into place if you remove some and drop it back into the mix. It's better to under-beat it than to over-beat it.

Spoon macaron batter into a pastry / frosting bag with a 1/4" or so opening – whether a metal tip, or just the end cut off the bag.

Pipe 1.25" – 1.5" rounds onto lined baking sheets. If the batter isn't running all over the place, there's no real worry about placing them close together – I'll leave an inch or so between the rounds.

Pick up the sheet of piped cookies, and rap it against the counter a couple of times to dislodge any air bubbles.

Bake cookies for 13-16 minutes, or until they lift easily from the parchment. (Undercooked macarons will stick). Remove from oven, cool to room temperature, and prepare the filling.

Orange-Lemon Buttercream Filling

Butter, softened	½ cup	125 ml
Orange, zest of	1	1
Lemon, zest of	1	1
Orange juice	1 Tbsp	15 ml
Powdered (confectioners / icing) sugar	1-2 cups	250-500 ml

Whip butter until smooth. Add zests and orange juice and mix until incorporated.

Slowly add 1 cup of powdered sugar a bit at a time, until incorporated completely. If mixture seems too thin, add a bit more powdered sugar, continuing to mix until thick (but spreadable!) and smooth.

To assemble Macarons

Spoon or pipe about a tablespoon worth of filling onto the flat underside of one cookie. Top with the underside of another cookie. (Rounded sides facing out). Holding cookies by the edge, twist gently to force frosting out almost to the edge.

Hop Meringues

Meringues are usually just sweet.. too sweet for my husband, as much fun as he finds them. (He likes to say meringues are like popping bubble wrap in your mouth - the bubbly texture as it crumbles and melts. I can see it.)

When it comes to these meringues, however, he can't get enough. The flavour of the hops cuts the "straight sugar" feeling of eating meringues, and brightens them up. These are refreshing, fun little crunchy cookies.

You CAN pipe these out into small rounds, or use a star shape tip to make "kisses", but we like to go all out and make hop shaped, hop flavoured meringues. Go big or go home, right?

Petal Dust and Pearl Dust can be purchased from any cake decorating supply store. They make great fake lupulin!

Makes about 40.

Large egg whites	3	3
Salt	1/4 tsp	1 ml
cream of tartar	1/4 tsp	1 ml
Granulated sugar	3/4 cup	175 ml
Hop extract	½ -1 tsp	2-5 ml
Green food colouring, optional		
Yellow or gold Petal Dust or Pearl Dust, optional		

Preheat oven to 185 F (85 C). Prepare cookie sheets by lining with parchment paper. (Do NOT use pan spray!)

In the bowl of a stand mixer, combine egg whites, salt, and cream of tartar. Using the whisk attachment, whip on high until glossy peaks form. Slowly add in the sugar – a little at a time – and continue whipping until stiff peaks form. Turn off mixer, remove bowl. Gently stir in hop extract to taste.

Tint with food colouring, if desired. Spoon meringue into a large pastry bag. You can fit the bag with a round tip before filling, if desired. If not using a tip, cut about 3/4" off the end of the bag to form a makeshift round tip,

Pipe a fat little log, about 1.5" long.

Starting at the point furthest away from you, use a toothpick to pull small amounts of meringue up and away from the main piped shape, to form a hop cone shape. (See next page for photos). Repeat to use up all of the meringue.

If desired, sprinkle meringues with Petal or Pearl dust

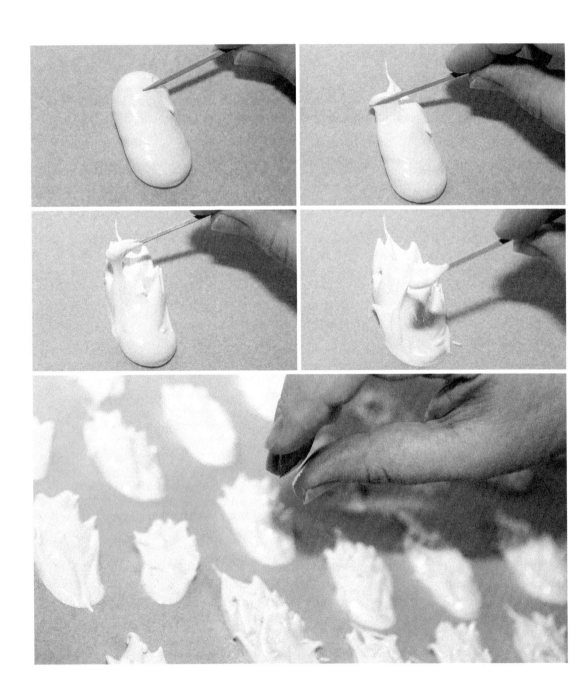

Bake for about 2 hours, or until just starting to get lightly browned. Once done, turn oven off, crack the door open and allow them to cool in the oven for several hours, before transferring to an airtight container.

Hop Meringues

Hop Chocolate

Beverages

Hop Chocolate

When the weather is miserable, sometimes it's nice to curl up with a mug of hot chocolate. I say "sometimes", because I'm one of those rare people who just isn't that much into chocolate.

So, when the mood does hit... I'm very "go big or go home" about it. I like to make my hot chocolate so ridiculously rich, that 1 coffee mug is enough. I would never be able to drink this in huge, gas station sized cups. It's diabetes in a cup! When it's cold and rainy, though - perfect. Feel free to thin it down with additional milk, if you'd like something a bit more … chuggable.

Of course, hot chocolate is even better when you add a little something - Irish cream, cinnamon, cayenne - it just finishes it off.

Earthy hops - like Fuggle - go especially well with hot chocolate. The chocolate tastes richer with the hops, almost like it as made with a more expensive chocolate. Classes it up, without actually tasting HOPPY. As the chocolate flavour fades away, you get a subtle remnant of hop flavour, a very pleasant layering of flavours.

Makes about 3 ½ cups

Cocoa powder	1/4 cup	50 ml
Brown sugar, packed	½ cup	125 ml
Salt	Pinch	Pinch
Hot water	1/4 cup	50 ml
Milk	3 cups	750 ml
Hop extract	1-2 tsp	5-10 ml

In a saucepan, whisk together cocoa, brown sugar, and salt. Add hot water, whisk to form a thick paste. Slowly add milk, whisking to fully incorporate it.

Bring the mixture up to just barely a simmer, stirring frequently. When hot enough, stir in extract - start with 1 tsp, adjust to taste - serve immediately!

Hop Liqueur

There are two main ways of making a liqueur.

The first - and most common, for home liqueur making - is slow infusion. With this method, you place your flavour ingredients in a vessel with high proof alcohol, and allow time to draw the flavours from the ingredients out into the spirit. It's strained, and then sweetened with a simple syrup.

For hop liqueur, I've found that a quick infusion tends to work best. With this method, you make a very flavourful syrup, cool it to room temperature, and then add alcohol. You'll still want to leave it for a little while to meld and mellow, but it's more or less good to go immediately. Huell Melon is my favourite variety for this.

This is a unique liqueur - distinctively hoppy, but balanced with sweetness and citrus. A great sippy drink for when you're in the mood for something different.

Makes 3 cups

Granulated sugar	1 1/4 cups	300 ml
Liquid honey	½ cup	125 ml
Water	1 cup	250 ml
Orange, peel of	1	1
Lemon, peel of	1	1
Lime, peel of	1	1
Salt	Pinch	Pinch
Powdered hop pellets	1 Tbsp	15 ml
Vodka	2 cups	500 ml

Combine sugar, honey, water, citrus peels, and salt in a saucepan. Heat to boiling, stirring until sugar is dissolved. Reduce heat to low and simmer for 10 minutes. Stir in hops, remove from heat and cool to room temperature.

Once cool, strain through a fine mesh strainer or cheese cloth, discard solids.

Stir about 1 ½ cups of vodka into the cooled syrup mixture, and taste. Continue adding vodka, to taste, until desired flavour / alcohol level is reached. Funnel into clean wine or liqueur bottles.

After bottling, you should let it age for about a week in a cool place before drinking it – IF you have that kind of patience! Aging results in a smoother, more mellow flavour.

Hop Liqueur

Hop Tea

Here's another recipe that's not so much a recipe, but ideas, inspiration, and loose guidelines.

Hop tea is a drink that's been made for hundreds of years, as a beverage and even as a medicine - hops are known for their calming, sedative effect, and even as an anti-inflammatory!

You can brew it strong using nothing but hops, or you can include other flavours for a more complex blend. You can use a French Press, tea ball, or bags. Fresh, dried, or pelletized hops ... see why writing an actual recipe doesn't make a ton of sense?

So, here are some basic guidelines:

Fresh Hops: Using a French press is the best way to make hop tea from fresh (wet) hops. Set your press up with a handful or so of fresh hops, top with almost-boiling water, and allow to steep for 3-5 minutes. Strain/press, and sweeten to taste.

Dried Hops: Dried hops can also be steeped in a French press, or can be crushed up and placed in a tea ball or tea bag.

Hop Pellets: Pellet hops shouldn't be used in a French press, as the material can gunk up the screen. Hop pellets can should be used whole in tea balls, or can be ground up for use in a tea bag.

Flavours: First of all - use a very low acid hop! Hop tea can get overwhelming pretty quickly, so don't stack the deck against yourself from the beginning. Under 5% alpha acid is ideal.

For add-ins, basically anything that you like in a normal tea blend can be added to hop tea! Try ginger (fresh or dried), citrus peels (fresh or dried), camomile, lemon grass, mint, lavender, rosehips, dried hibiscus - really, have fun with it!

Also, hop tea doesn't need to be completely made from scratch - you can heat up brewed hop tea and add a favourite commercial tea bag to it for a more traditional tea flavour.

Sweeteners: Sugar, brown sugar, agave, honey, maple syrup - you can sweeten hop tea the same ways you'd sweeten any other tea. Try to compliment the flavours of the tea!

Hop Tea

Lemonade

Lemonade is such an easy thing to make, and works SO well with a multitude of hop varieties. We prefer Citra® hops, but any citrus, fruity, or floral hops work really well for a complex, but still mostly traditional lemonade taste. Feel free to try other flavour profiles if desired! Because lemon works well with almost anything, you really can't go wrong using your favourite hop varieties.

Because the hop variety we prefer for lemonade is a high acid hop, this recipe includes a little baking soda, to tone it down a little. If you're using a low acid hop, feel free to skip the baking soda.

For single use lemonade, strain syrup into a jar, cover and refrigerate for up to two weeks. To serve, measure about 3 Tbsp of lemonade syrup into a tall class, top with cold water, and stir gently to combine.

If you'd like to use fresh hops for this, use about 1 oz.

Makes about 2L finished lemonade

Water	1 cup	250 ml
Granulated sugar	1 cup	250 ml
Lemon, zest of	1	1
Salt	Pinch	Pinch
Baking soda	1/4 tsp	1 ml
Dried hops - leaves or pellets	½ oz	15 g
Freshly squeezed lemon juice	1 cup	250 ml
Cold water		

In a medium saucepan, combine water, sugar, and lemon zest. Bring to a boil over medium heat, stirring to dissolve sugar.

Once sugar is dissolved, add baking soda and hops. Stir and remove from heat. Cover and allow to steep for 10 minutes.

When 10 minutes is up, add lemon juice and stir well. Pour through a cheesecloth lined strainer (I find 2 or 3 layers of cheesecloth works best), and into a 2L (½ gallon) sized pitcher. Discard hop pulp.

Add cold water to pitcher - to taste - stir well, and allow to chill for 30 minutes before serving.

Lemonade

145

Malted Milkshake

Here is another case where hops bring a lot of complexity to something, without really announcing themselves as HOPS.

In this milkshake, the hops really enhance the vanilla, making it seem more intense. It almost works like salt does in this case, making flavours seem like MORE of themselves.

The malt extract adds sweetness and character, and balances out the hop. It uses two of the cornerstone ingredients/ profiles of beer - the malt and the hops - without tasting anything at all like beer.

We like using a low acid, earthy hop extract for this - fresh, dry, and pelletized hops just don't work as well for this recipe. Fuggle is my favourite in this recipe.

Makes 1 serving

Vanilla ice cream	1 cup	250 ml
Milk	½ -1 cup	125-250 ml
Dry malt extract (DME)	2 Tbsp	30 ml
Hop extract	1 tsp	5 ml

Measure all ingredients into a blender, blitz until smooth and well combined. If you like milkshakes a little thinner, add more milk.

Serve immediately.

Variations: Chocolate and/or coffee ice cream makes a great substitute for vanilla in this recipe.

Malted Milkshake

Hop Soda

Quick Hop Soda

Hop Soda is very easy to make, yet very versatile and fun to play with. This base soda syrup cooks up in just minutes, and can be used to make a hopped cream soda or any number of other flavours. This can be used in a soda machine, or just enjoyed as a quick soda mix, a little at a time.

For hops, we like to use something fruity, usually Amarillo®... but feel free to use your favourite variety. If you'd like to use fresh hops, use about 1 oz.

A note on sweetness: 2 cups of sugar creates a dry soda, 2 ½ cups of sugar a more sweet one. If you like sodas VERY sweet, you can use even more sugar, to taste.

Makes about 2 cups of syrup

Water	1 ½ cups	375 ml
Granulated sugar	2-2 ½ cups	500-550 ml
Salt	Pinch	Pinch
Baking soda	1/4 tsp	1 tsp
Dried hops - leaves or pellets	½ oz	15 g
Carbonated water, Seltzer Water, etc		

In a medium saucepan, combine water, sugar and salt. Bring to a boil over medium heat, stirring to dissolve sugar. Once sugar is dissolved, add baking soda and hops. Stir and remove from heat. Cover and allow to steep for 10 minutes.

Once the steeping time is finished, pour through a cheesecloth lined strainer (I find 2 or 3 layers of cheesecloth works best), and into a clean jar. Discard hop pulp. Cover and refrigerate for up to two weeks

To use: Measure about 3 Tbsp soda syrup into a tall glass, top with carbonated/seltzer water, and stir gently to combine. Alternately, soda syrup can be used in soda machines, in place of store bought syrups.

To force carbonate it, if you have the equipment: Make 6-8x batch of syrup, for 5 gallon keg. Top with distilled water. Seal off keg and carbonate per your set up.

Variations:

Hoppy cream soda: Add 1 Tbsp vanilla extract to cooled syrup, stir well to combine.

Fresh fruit: Add a cup of berries or fruit puree and/or a bit of citrus zest to the initial boil of sugar and water.

Floral: Depending on hop variety, floral flavoured sodas can be fun. Add a handful of fresh rose petals or a little dried lavendar to the initial boil of syrup.

Brewed Hop Soda

If you yearn for the taste of brewed sodas, this is a unique recipe for you. Brewing soda takes a bit more commitment than the preceding recipe, but produces the characteristic flavours of old fashioned, brewed soda.

We like to use Centennial hops for this recipe, but most/all varieties would work well. Go with what you like! If you'd like to use fresh hops, use about 1 oz. Use distilled or otherwise bottled water - tap water can impart weird flavours on the finished drink.

Makes 2 L

Water, divided	8 cups	2 L
Granulated sugar	1 1/4 cup	300 ml
Salt	Pinch	Pinch
Baking soda	1/4 tsp	1 tsp
Dried hops - leaves or pellets	½ oz	15 g
Bread yeast	1/4 tsp	1 ml

In a medium saucepan, combine 2 cups of water, sugar and salt. Bring to a boil over medium heat, stirring to dissolve sugar. Once sugar is dissolved, add baking soda and hops. Stir and remove from heat. Cover and allow to steep for 10 minutes.

When 10 minutes is up, pour through a cheesecloth lined strainer (I find 2 or 3 layers of cheesecloth works best), discarding hop pulp. Use a funnel to transfer cooled soda syrup to a clean 2L pop bottle. Add yeast and about 1 cup of water to the bottle, swirl to combine. Top with remaining water, leaving about 1" empty head space in the bottle. Cap tightly.

Allow bottle to sit at room temperature for 1-3 days, just until the bottle gets hard (pressurized!) from the carbonation that is building inside. Chill pressurized bottle upright in the fridge for a few days, allowing the yeast to settle on the bottom of the bottle.

To serve, gentle pour from the bottle, taking care not to disturb the settled yeast. When you get down to the last bit of soda in the bottle, discard it along with the yeast.

Variations:

Hoppy cream soda:	Add 1 Tbsp vanilla extract to cooled syrup before adding yeast, stir well to combine.
Fresh fruit:	Add a cup of berries or fruit puree and/or a bit of citrus zest to the initial boil of sugar and water.
Floral:	Depending on your hop variety, floral flavoured sodas can be fun. Add a handful of fresh rose petals or a little dried lavendar to the initial boil of sugar and water

Hopped Hard Apple Cider

Hard cider is one of those things that we tend to kind of... wing. A lot of it is taste, instinct, etc. Some apple ciders are sweeter than others, or have a particular flavour that would work really well with a certain hop, or whatever. Sometimes we're in the mood for a rich, caramel flavoured brown sugar cider, sometimes more in the mood for making a cider sweetened with granulated sugar - letting the true apple flavour shine more, in a lighter cider.

While traditional cider makes use of many potential optional ingredients - cinnamon, nutmeg, cloves, molasses, maple syrup , raisins, etc - we tend to avoid those when making hopped cider. Sometimes we'll use a little honey as part of the sugar, sometimes we'll include a small amount of citrus peel - but that's about it.

We prefer to dry hop cider, as boiling the cider isn't a good idea in general. As far as hop selection goes, we like to use hops that are citrussy, floral, or grassy

You want your apple cider to be preservative free. This is absolutely key! If the cider you purchase has anything like sodium benzoate, potassium sorbate, etc, your yeast will not be able to ferment it. Worst case scenario, most grocery stores will carry a pasteurized apple cider in plastic bottles, near the apple juice. Go for it!

We like Red Star brand "Cote de Blancs" yeast for making cider, but most will work. Yeast can and will affect the outcome of your cider, so if you haven't worked with it before, I'd suggest reading up before choosing!

Makes about 5 gallons

Apple cider	5 gallons	20 L
Granulated sugar*	5-10 lbs	2 1/4- 4 ½ kg
Wine yeast	2 packets	2 packets
Dried or Pellet hops	1-2 oz	30-55 g

In large stock pot, combine apple cider with the sugar. Heat to almost boiling, stirring until sugar is dissolved. Continue to heat for about 45 minutes – never allowing it to come to a boil. Remove from heat, cover with sanitized pot lid. (If you don't have a 7-10 gallon stock pot or turkey fryer, you can do this in batches.)

Once mixture has cooled to room temperature, use a sanitized funnel to transfer cooled mixture to a sanitized 6.5-7.5 gallon fermenter.

Sprinkle yeast into fermenter, cover with sanitized air lock. Let sit, undisturbed, overnight.

Within 48 hours, you should notice fermentation activity – bubbles in the airlock, carbonation and /or swirling in the cider must. This means you're good to go! Put the carboy somewhere cool (not cold!), and leave it alone for a month or so.

Place your hops in a freshly sanitized fermenter bucket. Rack the cider off the sediment in the initial fermenter, into this new bucket. Swirl, cover and leave it alone for anywhere from a few days, to 2-3 weeks. If you taste to see when you want to take it off the hops, be sure to use sanitized equipment to remove the sample!

Once you're happy with the flavour, rack the cider off the hops and into a freshly sanitized 5 gallon carboy. Cap with sanitized airlock, leave it alone for another 2-3 months.

When you've let it clarify as much as you have patience for – with no more sediment being produced – you can move on to bottling:

For uncarbonated cider:

Using sanitized equipment, take a final gravity reading, then rack the cider into clean, sanitized beer bottles, and cap them. Allow to age for a month or so before drinking. (Like wine, the flavour improves with age!)

For naturally carbonated cider:

In a small pot, mix together 1 cup of water with 1 cup of sugar or brown sugar. Use a sanitized funnel to pour this into a sanitized large carboy. Rack the cider over into this carboy, swirling it as you go. Bottle cider as described in the previous step. Allow to age at least a month or two – residual yeast will ferment the added sugar, carbonating the cider.

Alternatively, you can rack the cider (without the added sugar syrup!) into a keg and force carbonate it, if you have the set up for that.

*While sugar is technically optional, NOT adding any sugar will result in a very, very dry cider. Any amount of sugar will result in a higher alcohol content. At around 7 lbs, you should have a good, semi sweet cider.

Hopped Hard Apple Cider

Hopped Orange Mead

154

Hopped Orange Mead

The very first mead recipe we ever created, quickly became the mead recipe that all of our other batches are based on. It was just that good - but hey, we made it from Christmas clementine oranges, so...

For a hopped mead, we decided to keep the citrus profile of that original mead, but open it up to using oranges that are more easy to find year round. If you have access to clementines, by all means - use them! Choose hops that work well with the flavour of the oranges - citrus, tropical, or grassy hops work best.

Because this is a sweet mead, it's very good even when fairly "young". Compared to many drier meads – At only 6 months old, this tastes amazing. That's a good thing, as we don't have to worry so much about a race between aging a mead to taste good, vs not letting it age so much that the hop flavour degrades. Wider windows of drinkability are a good thing!

The ABV on this tends to come out to about 8%. Unlike cider making, which we freestyle and end up with flavour profiles and ABV readings all over the place, we tend to follow this recipe specifically, with much more predictable results. We use White Labs "WLP 720 Sweet Mead" yeast for this. You can use others, but it will change your final results a bit.

Makes about 5 gallons

Spring water	4 gallons	15 L
Liquid honey	15 lbs	6.5 kg
Vanilla beans, split lengthwise	2	2
Oranges, peels and juice of	12	12
Acid blend	1 tsp	5 ml
Yeast nutrient	3 tsp	15 ml
Yeast	1 packet	1 packet
Dried or Pellet hops	1-2 oz	30-55 g

Heat 3 gallons of the water to a simmer. Add honey, stir until dissolved.

Add vanilla beans (scraping seeds into the mixture before adding the pods), peels, and juice. Bring mixture back up to a simmer and keep it there – just simmering, not boiling – for about 45 minutes. Stir in acid blend and yeast nutrient.

Strain mixture into a sanitized bucket, removing fruit peels and vanilla beans. Cover bucket with sanitized lid, allow to cool to room temperature.

Using a sanitized funnel, transfer cooled mixture to a sanitized 5 gallon carboy, topping up with remaining water until carboy is almost full. Swirl to combine.

Sprinkle yeast into carboy, cover with sanitized air lock. Let sit, undisturbed, overnight.

Within 24 hours, you should notice fermentation activity – bubbles in the airlock, carbonation and /or swirling in the mead must. This means you're good to go! Put the carboy somewhere cool (not cold!), and leave it alone for a month.

Place your hops in a freshly sanitized fermenter bucket. Rack the mead off the sediment in the initial fermenter, into this new bucket. Swirl, cover and leave it alone for anywhere from a few days, to 2-3 weeks. If you taste to see when you want to take it off the hops, be sure to use sanitized equipment to remove the sample!

Once you're happy with the flavour, rack the mead off the hops and into a freshly sanitized 5 gallon carboy. Cap with sanitized airlock, leave it alone for another 2-3 months.

Repeat racking process. Leave mead alone for a month or two. By 6 months in, your mead should be very clear, and VERY tasty!

When you've let it clarify as much as you have patience for – with no more sediment being produced – you can move on to bottling:

Using sanitized equipment, rack the mead into clean, sanitized bottles. Cork. (We like to "Zorks" for corking our homemade wine. Easy to use – no special equipment needed! – easy to uncork, and – should you have any wine left in your bottle after serving, the "cork" is easily replaced for temporary storage!)

Alternately, feel free to force carbonate this in a keg setup. Sparkling mead feels so.. Fancy!

Bitters

A few years ago, my husband and I had some grand ideas about putting out a line of hopped bitters. There was nothing like that available at the time, and we had some fun ideas for playing off the notes in a few main varieties of hops. We registered a name, a domain, designed a logo and came up with some recipes... and then got busy and didn't bother going any further with it. Boo! Now there are several commercially available hopped bitters on the market.

Bitters are basically like an extract, but stronger and - surprise! - much more bitter. There are all kind of things used as bittering agents in any of the many varieties of bitters out there, but we like to use hops. Not only do they have a wide variety of flavours available, but each hop variety adds a complex, multifaceted taste that you just can't get from most individual bittering ingredients alone.

We tend to gravitate towards the more fruity, citrussy flavours, and then play it up with the aromatics we add. A lemon-orangey hop with the addition of citrus peels adds several layers of not only citrus flavour, but green, vegetal notes as well - bright and clean tasting.

Fair warning : what we have here is another "not really a recipe"-recipe!

Much like liqueurs, there are two main ways to make bitters: Slow infusion, and a quicker boil followed by adding alcohol.

Slower infusion works well with many traditional bittering ingredients, but extracting the bitterness and aroma from hops - for this kind of use - requires isomerization. Thus: They should be boiled.

For the most complex hop flavour, making bitters in a two step process - both wet hopping (boil) and dry hopping (infusion) is best. Here's a good base recipe for hop bitters:

Water	1 ½ cups	375 ml
Bittering Hops	1 oz	30 g
Aroma Hops	1/4-½ oz	7.5-15 g
Overproof Alcohol*	1 cup	250 ml

In a medium sized pot, bring water to a boil. Add bittering hops, reduce heat to low, and stir well. Cover pot and allow to simmer for 20 minutes.

Place aroma hops into a clean - ideally sterilized - container. Strain water through 2-3 layers of cheesecloth, over aroma hops. Seal tightly, store in a cool dark place for 5 days, shaking daily.

Strain bitters out through layered cheesecloth one final time. Taste, add more alcohol if you need to tone down the intensity of the hop bitterness.

Bottle bitters into small dark glass bottles - ideally with eyedroppers affixed to the caps.

Use in your favourite bitters-containing cocktail recipe, or add a couple drops to a bit of white rum or tequila for a hoppy flavour boost

* A note on alcohol: Generally speaking, overproof grain alcohol is best for this - usually Everclear. This is because you want to set off the water content added by boiling the hops.

Using a high proof alcohol leaves you with more actual alcohol after that point, than you'd have if you were using regular vodka. This is a good thing, when making bitters - it'll put you closer to the alcohol level of normal, unboiled bitters.

If you don't have access to high proof alcohol where you live, use the highest proof vodka you can find.

Adding Other Flavours

While straight hop bitters can be great, you're missing out on a ton of the potential of layering flavours.

You can flavour your hops with all kinds of non-hop aromatics - Citrus peels, peppercorns, herbs, dried spices - like cinnamon sticks, whole cloves, or star anise - juniper berries, dried flowers, home brewing wood cubes (for finishing), and more.

HOW you get those flavours into your bitters fall into 4 main techniques. You can more or less use whichever you want - they'll all produce slightly different results, though.

In the boil	Add your aromatics in the initial boil, along with the hops. This is a great way to extract the maximum flavour from your aromatics, but doesn't give you a lot of control.
Infusion:	Add your aromatics to the mix while infusing the aromatic hops. Again, this method is less work, but doesn't allow for a lot of control with the ingredients.
After Infusion:	Add the aromatics after the hop infusion. When using more than one kind of non-hop aromatic, you can do them all at once, or start with one ingredient, then customize. For example, you can infuse orange peels until it tastes great, strain that out. Add, say, peppercorns next... and so on. It gives you more control over individual flavour profiles.
Separate Infusions:	Finally, for the MOST control, you can mix infusions. Start with not only your main, basic hop infusion.. But separate infusions of other flavours. You might have a small bottle of alcohol that's been infused with orange peel for a few months, and another that's been soaking oak cubes for a while. You add the separate flavours to your hop infusion, little by little, tinkering until you're happy with the mix. Maximum control!

Hop Bitters

159

Sour Mix

This goes by a few names – "bar lime", "bar mix", "sweet and sour", etc – and is a versatile ingredient to have available for your home bar. We like to make about a liter of it at a time, keeping it in a bottle in the fridge. It's really convenient! Sour mix is not only used for, well, SOURS, but is also used as an ingredient in many cocktails, and is the foundational flavour in a margarita. Trust me, once you make your own, you'll never want to buy the premade stuff again!

Hopped sour mix has a subtle but distinct complexity that you don't find in even homemade sour mix - an easy way to elevate a simple drink! We like Kent Goulding in this recipe, but most citrus or floral hop varieties would work well. This recipe can be scaled up or down, as needed. Also, while the proportion of lemon/lime here is traditional, feel free to play with it, or add different citrus fruits for a more complex flavour.

Makes about 3 cups

Water	1 ½ cups	375 ml
Dried hop leaves	1/3 cup	75 ml
Granulated sugar	1 ½ cups	375 ml
Freshly squeezed lemon juice	1 cup	250 ml
Freshly squeezed lime juice	1 cup	250 ml

Combine water and hops in a medium saucepan. Bring just to a simmer, remove from heat and allow to steep for 10 minutes. Strain, discard hops.

Add sugar to saucepan, return to heat. Cook, stirring just until sugar is dissolved. Remove from heat, cool.

Once syrup has cooled, add lemon and lime juices, stir well. Store unused syrup in the fridge for no more than 2 weeks.

"Sours" Cocktails

Liquor/liqueur of choice*	1 oz	30 g
Sour mix		

Fill a rocks glass with ice – ice should come just above the edge of the glass. Pour liquor/liqueur over the ice, top up with sour mix, and pour glass contents into a shaker. Shake, then pour contents back into the rocks glass. (Usually, I skip the shaker and just stir it!)

* Amaretto, Drambuie, Whiskey, Tequila, Scotch, and Vodka are all popular

Sour Mix Cocktail

Conversions

To accommodate bakers in different countries and from different cultures, measurements throughout this book have been provided in both U.S. conventional and metric. To keep things simple, measurement conversions have been rounded. See below for the exact conversions, as well as the rounded versions provided throughout this book.

Spoons	Actual Conversion*	Standard Metric Used
1/4 tsp	1.2 ml	1 ml
½ tsp	2.5 ml	2 ml
1 tsp	4.9 ml	5 ml
1 Tbsp	14.8 ml	15 ml

Cups	Actual Conversion*	Standard Metric Used
1/4 cup	59.1 ml	50 ml
1/3 cup	78.9 ml	75 ml
½ cup	118.3 ml	125 ml
2/3 cup	157.7 ml	150 ml
3/4 cup	177.4 ml	175 ml
1 cup	236.6 ml	250 ml
4 cups	946.4 ml	1000 ml / 1 liter

Ounces (Weight)	Actual Conversion*	Standard Metric Used
1 oz	28.3 grams	30 grams
2 oz	56.7 grams	55 grams
3 oz	85.0 grams	85 grams
4 oz	113.4 grams	125 grams
5 oz	141.7 grams	140 grams
6 oz	170.1 grams	170 grams
7 oz	198.4 grams	200 grams
8 oz	226.8 grams	250 grams
16 oz / 1 lb	453.6 grams	500 grams
32 oz / 2 lbs	907.2 grams	1000 grams / 1 kilogram

* Source: Google Calculator

Resources

This list is for informational purposes only, and does not necessarily constitute an endorsement of any of these companies. We do not receive payment of any kind by these companies for being listed here. It is the readers' responsibility to properly vet any companies they choose to do business with; we are not responsible for any disputes that may arise.

For hops, hop rhizomes, and home brewing supplies, it's best to search for what's local to you, or delivers to your area, specifically.

Equipment and Supplies

Amazon
www.amazon.com
Glass dropper bottles for bitters, stand up pouches for packaging dried hops, "Zork" corks for homebrewing, etc.

Specialty Bottle
www.specialtybottle.com
Glass dropper bottles for bitters.

Unline
www.uline.com
Stand up pouches for packaging dried hops.

Ingredients

Amazon
www.amazon.com
Gluten-free flours

Pimento Wood
www.pimentowood.com
Pimento wood, leaves, etc for making proper Jerk BBQ.

Nuts Online
www.nutsonline.com
Nuts, gluten-free flours, and more.

Other

Celebration Generation
www.celebrationgeneration.com
Food & lifestyle blog, recipes, photos, cookbooks, and inspiration.

Index

Marie Porter

Marie Porter is an Aspergian polymath, which is just a fancy way of saying that she knows a lot of stuff - and does even more stuff - with a brain that runs on a different operating system than most. Because of that OS, her career has spanned across many facets: She's a trained mixologist, competitive cake artist, professional costumer, and - last but not least - author. As of 2016, her written works include 6 cookbooks, 6 specialty sewing manuals, and a tornado memoir. Her work has graced magazines and blogs around the world, she has costumed for Olympians and professional wrestlers, has baked for brides, celebrities, and even Klingons. Marie is now proud to share her wealth of multi-disciplinary knowledge and experience with cooks and seamstresses around the world.

Michael Porter

Michael Porter works in medical manufacturing, and is a food and commercial photographer. His work has appeared in local, national, and international magazines, in catalogs, corporate websites, and as well as in many online media outlets. In addition to being an awesome husband and photographer, Michael is Celebration Generation's "Chief Engineering Officer", responsible for all custom builds, equipment repairs, and warp engine emergencies. After their home was smashed by a tornado, Michael singlehandedly built all of the cabinetry in their new kitchen! In his 'spare' time, Michael is an avid home brewer, and is pursuing a degree in engineering".

MARIE PORTER

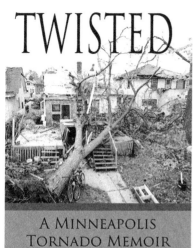

Twisted: A Minneapolis Tornado Memoir

On the afternoon of May 22, 2011, North Minneapolis was devastated by a tornado. Twisted recounts the Porters' first 11 months, post tornado. Rebuilding their house, working around the challenges presented by inadequate insurance coverage. Frustration at repeated bouts of incompetence and greed from their city officials. Dealing with issues such as loss of control, logistics, change, and over-stimulation, as two adults with Aspergers. With the help of social media – and the incredibly generous support of the geek community – the Porters were able to emerge from the recovery marathon without too much of a hit to their sanity levels. New friends were made, new skills learned, and a "new" house emerged from the destruction. Twisted is a roller coaster of emotion, personal observations, rants, humor, social commentary, set backs and triumphs. Oh, and details on how to cook jambalaya for almost 300 people, in the parking lot of a funeral home… should you ever find yourself in the position to do so!

The Spirited Baker
Intoxicating Desserts & Potent Potables

Combining liqueurs with more traditional baking ingredients can yield spectacular results. Try Mango Mojito Upside Down Cake, Candy Apple Flan, Jalapeno Beer Peanut Brittle, Lynchburg Lemonade Cupcakes, Pina Colada Rum Cake, Strawberry Daiquiri Chiffon Pie, and so much more.

To further add to your creative possibilities, the first chapter teaches how to infuse spirits to make both basic & cream liqueurs, as well as home made flavor extracts! This book contains over 160 easy to make recipes, with variation suggestions to help create hundreds more!

Evil Cake Overlord
Ridiculously Delicious Cakes

Marie Porter has been known for her "ridiculously delicious" moist cakes and tasty, unique flavors since the genesis of her custom cake business. Now, you can have recipes for all of the amazing flavors on her former custom cake menu, as well as many more! Once you have baked your moist work of gastronomic art, fill & frost your cake with any number of tasty possibilities. Milk chocolate cardamom pear, mango mojito.. even our famous Chai cake – the flavor that got us into "Every Day with Rachel Ray" magazine! Feeling creative? Use our easy to follow recipe to make our yummy fondant. Forget everything you've heard about fondant – ours is made from marshmallows and powdered sugar, and is essentially candy – you can even flavor it to bring a whole new level of "yum!" to every cake you make!

Beyond Flour
A Fresh Approach to Gluten-Free Cooking & Baking

Most gf recipes are developed by taking a "normal" recipe, swapping in a simulated "all purpose" gluten-free flour… whether store bought, or a homemade version. "Beyond Flour" takes a bit of a different approach: developing the recipe from scratch. Rather than just swapping out the flour for an "all purpose" mix, Marie Porter uses various alternative flours as individual ingredients – skillfully blending flavours, textures, and other properties unique to each flour – not making use of any kind of all-purpose flour mix. Supporting ingredients and different techniques are also utilized to achieve the perfect end goal … not just a "reasonable facsimile". With Beyond Flour, you can now indulge in some of your deepest, darkest guilty pleasure food cravings -safely and joyously!

Hedonistic Hops
The HopHead's Guide to Kitchen Badassery

While hops may seem like a bizarre or exotic item to cook with, they're really not that different from any other herb or spice in your cupboard… you just have to know what to do with them! From condiments, sides, & main dishes, to beverages and desserts, Marie Porter creates delicious recipes utilizing hops of various flavour profiles - playing up their unique characteristics - to create recipes full of complex flavour. Much like salt or lemon juice can be added to dishes to perk them up, a small amount of hops - used wisely, and with specific techniques to do so in a balanced fashion - can really make a dish sing. Even those who are not fans of beer will love the unique flavours that various types of hops can bring to their plate. Floral, earthy, peppery, citrusy… Cooking with hops is a great way to expand your seasoning arsenal!

Beyond Flour 2
A Fresh Approach to Gluten-Free Cooking & Baking

How many times have you come across a gluten-free recipe claiming to be "just as good as the normal version!", only to find that the author must have had some skewed memories on what the "normal" version tasted, looked, and/or felt like? How many times have you felt the need to settle for food with weird after-taste, gummy consistency, or cardboard-like texture, convinced that this is your new lot in life?

Continuing where its predecessor left off, "Beyond Flour 2"is full of tasty gluten-free recipes that have been developed from scratch to be the absolute best they can be - as good or better than the "real" thing - with no "all purpose" mixes, and no need to compromise on taste or texture!

Sweet Corn Spectacular
(Minnesota Historical Society Press)

The height of summer brings with it the bounty of fresh sweet corn Grilled or boiled, slathered in butter and sprinkled with salt, corn on the cob is a mainstay of cook-out menus. But this "vegetable" can grace your plate in so many other ways. In fact, author and baker Marie Porter once devised an entire day's worth of corn-based dishes to celebrate her "corn freak"husband's birthday. "Sweet Corn Spectacular" displays Porter's creative and flavor-filled approach to this North American original, inspiring year-round use of this versatile ingredient and tasty experimenting in your own kitchen. As Porter reminds home cooks, the possibilities are endless!

Introducing Marie Porter's "Spandex Simplified" Series

Prior to her recipe development career, Marie Porter had an illustrious career in spandex costuming. Now, you can learn all of her secrets to spandex design and sewing!

"Synchro Swimwear", "Sewing for Skaters", "Sewing for Gymnasts", "Fitness & Bodybuilding", "Sewing for Superheroes", and "Custom Swimwear" are the first six titles in Marie's Spandex Simplified series, and are all about designing and creating spectacular and durable competitive and recreational sports apparel and costuming. "Sewing for Dancers" is scheduled for a 2017 release.

These books are appropriate for beginner to advanced levels of sewing ability, and are written from both a designer, and former "performance" athlete's point of view. They teach everything from the basics, to tricks of the trade. The "Spandex Simplified" series will prepare the reader to design and make almost any design of competitive synchro suit, skating dress, gymnastics leotard, posing suit, swimsuit, or spandex cosplay imaginable.

Given the cost of decent custom spandex garments, these manuals each pay for themselves with the savings from just one project!

The books are written completely in laymans' terms and carefully explained, step by step. Only basic sewing knowledge and talent is required. Learn everything from measuring and pattern alteration, to easily creating ornate applique designs, and embellishing the finished suit in one book!

For complete Tables of Contents, more info, and to order, visit
www.spandexsimplified.com

To order any or all of Celebration Generation's titles, visit us online at
www.celebrationgeneration.com

CPSIA information can be obtained
at www.ICGtesting.com
Printed in the USA
BVOW07s2132090616

451467BV00008B/10/P